Life-Centered Economic System

# *Toward a Life-Centered Economy: From the Rule of Money to the Rewards of Stewardship*

Money-Centered Economic System

## QIF Focus Books

1–*Fueling our Future: A Dialogue about Technology, Ethics, Public Policy, and Remedial Action,* coordinated by Ed Dreby and Keith Helmuth, edited by Judy Lumb, 2009.

2–*How on Earth Do We Live Now? Natural Capital, Deep Ecology, and the Commons,* by David Ciscel, Barbara Day, Keith Helmuth, Sandra Lewis, and Judy Lumb, 2011.

3–*Genetically Modified Crops: Promises, Perils, and the Need for Public Policy,* by Anne Mitchell, with Pinayur Rajagopal, Keith Helmuth, and Susan Holtz, 2011.

4–*How Does Societal Transformation Happen? Values Development, Collective Wisdom, and Decision Making for the Common Good,* by Leonard Joy, 2011.

5–*It's the Economy, Friends: Understanding the Growth Dilemma,* edited by Ed Dreby, Keith Helmuth, and Margaret Mansfield, 2012.

6–*Beyond the Growth Dilemma: Toward an Ecologically Integrated Economy,* edited by Ed Dreby and Judy Lumb, 2012.

7–*A Quaker Approach to Research: Collaborative Practice and Communal Discernment,* by Gray Cox with Charles Blanchard, Geoff Garver, Keith Helmuth, Leonard Joy, Judy Lumb, and Sara Wolcott, 2014.

8–*Climate, Food and Violence: Understanding the Connections, Exploring Responses,* by Judy Lumb, Phil Emmi, Mary Gilbert, Laura Holliday, Leonard Joy, and Shelley Tanenbaum, 2014.

9–*Toward a Right Relationship with Finance: Debt, Interest, Growth, and Security,* by Pamela Haines, Ed Dreby, David Kane, Charles Blanchard, 2016.

10–*Rising to the Challenge: The Transition Movement and People of Faith,* by Ruah Swennerfelt, 2016.

11–*Energy Choices: Opportunities to Make Wise Decisions for a Sustainable Future,* by Robert Bruninga with Judy Lumb, Frank Granshaw, and Charles Blanchard, 2018.

12–*Toward a Life-Centered Economy: From the Rule of Money to the Rewards of Stewardship,* by John Lodenkamper, Paul Alexander, Pete Baston, and Judith Streit, 2019.

# *Toward a Life-Centered Economy:*
## *From the Rule of Money to the Rewards of Stewardship*

*John Lodenkamper,*
*Paul Alexander,*
*Pete Baston, and*
*Judith Streit*

*QIF Focus Book 12*

*Quaker Institute for the Future 2019*

Published for Quaker Institute for the Future by *Producciones de la Hamaca*, Caye Caulker, Belize <producciones-hamaca.com>
ISBN: 978-976-8273-11-6 (paperback) and
ISBN: 978-976-8273-12-3 (e-book)

*Toward a Life-Centered Economy: From the Rule of Money to the Rewards of Stewardship* is the twelth in the series of *QIF Focus Books*
ISBN: 978-976-8142-90-0
(formerly *Quaker Institute for the Future Pamphlets*)

Unless otherwise indicated, all illustrations are by Pete Baston.

This book was printed on-demand by Lightning Source, Inc (LSI). The on-demand printing system is environmentally friendly because books are printed as needed, instead of in large numbers that might end up in someone's basement or a dump site. In addition, LSI is committed to using materials obtained by sustainable forestry practices. LSI is certified by Sustainable Forestry Initiative (SFI® Certificate Number: PwC-SFICOC-345 SFI-00980). The Sustainable Forestry Initiative is an independent, internationally recognized non-profit organization responsible for the SFI certification standard, the world's largest single forest certification standard. The SFI program is based on the premise that responsible environmental behavior and sound business decisions can co-exist to the benefit of communities,

***QIF Focus Books*** aim to provide critical information and understanding born of careful discernment on social, economic, and ecological realities, inspired by the testimonies and values of the Religious Society of Friends (Quakers). We live in a time when social and ecological issues are converging toward catastrophic breakdown. Human adaptation to social, economic and planetary realities must be re-thought and re-designed. ***QIF Focus Books*** are dedicated to this calling based on a spiritual and ethical commitment to right relationship with Earth's whole commonwealth of life. <quakerinstitute.org>

***Producciones de la Hamaca*** is dedicated to:

—Celebration and documentation of Earth and all her inhabitants,
—Restoration and conservation of Earth's natural resources,
—Creative expression of the sacredness of Earth and Spirit.

## *Contents*

# *List of Acronyms*

AI - Artificial Intelligence

BBC—British Broadcasting Company

CDO—Collateralized Debt Obligations

CSA—Community Supported Agriculture

CTC—Cradle to Cradle, i.e. circular economic production

DRC—Democratic Republic of Congo

E.S.G.—Environmental, Social and corporate Governance issues, as in socially responsible investing

FCC—Federal Communications Commission

GDP—Gross Domestic Product

GEO—Grassroots Economics Organization

GHG—Greenhouse gas

GMO—Genetically Modified Organism

GNI—Gross National Income

GPI—Genuine Progress Indicator

HDI—Human Development Index

IWI—Inclusive Wealth Index

MOOC—Massive Online Open Courses

MPGge—Miles Per Gallon gasoline equivalent

QR—Quick Response black and white product codes

STEM—Science, Technology, Engineering and Math, as in education

US—United States

# Preface

This twelfth *QIF Focus Book* was prepared by a Circle of Discernment, a small research group under the auspices of the Quaker Institute for the Future.[1] It builds on *QIF Focus Book #6, Beyond the Growth Dilemma: Toward an Ecologically Integrated Economy*.[2] The inspiration for this work came from an essay by Alan N. Connor, "Restructuring the Economy,"[3] which envisions a re-localized economic system as a subset of the natural ecological system.

We seek to address the fundamental problem of a global economic system that is predicated on unlimited growth, but resides within Earth's ecosystem that has limited natural resources and limited capacity to absorb pollution. Our primary audience is the US since the global reach of its advertising and entertainment media has promoted a materialistic, consumption-oriented lifestyle that is unsustainable, and it is therefore incumbent upon us in the US to promote a viable alternative.

We envision a realistic paradigm shift to a Life-Centered Economy that not only enables a higher quality of human life for everyone, but also provides for the long-term life of the ecosystem.

We lift up a reorientation toward seeking "Quality of Life" rather than "Quantity of Stuff."

Chapter 1 focuses on a shift in values toward how we spend our time, rather than seeking ever more money for material goods at the expense of what really matters in life. In Chapter 2 we re-imagine the current Money-Centered Economy as a Life-Centered Economy, and show the foundational values that support this alternative as well as some practical aspects of such a transformation. Chapter 3 elaborates on the synergism in the Life-Centered Economy, as seen through the lens of the human household.

In Chapter 4, a range of practical means for transition to a Life-Centered Economy are offered. And finally, in Chapter 5, we raise the challenge for a way forward that provides realistic paths to the critically needed changes for the good of all on Earth.

Our work was preceded by a Quaker Institute for the Future interest group formed by Elaine and Rich Andrews of Boulder Friends Meeting in Boulder, Colorado. This in turn led to an initial Circle of Discernment that included Elaine Andrews and Pete Baston of Boulder Friends Meeting and Paul Alexander and John Lodenkamper of Mountain View Friends Meeting in Denver, Colorado. John Lodenkamper has served as clerk of this Circle of Discernment.

We also benefited from a second circle of reviewers that initially included Linda Lodenkamper, Elsa Sabath, Libby Comeaux, Alan Connor and Judy Lumb, our editor and publisher. Over time the composition of both groups has changed, with Elaine Andrews moving to the circle of reviewers and being replaced by Dick Williams of Boulder Friends Meeting, who sharpened our knowledge of cooperatives before retiring. He in turn was replaced by Judith Streit of Mountain View Friends Meeting. Additions to the circle of reviewers include Laura Holliday, Leonard Joy, Charles Blanchard, Pamela Haines, and Nancy Dunkle.

—John Lodenkamper, Paul Alexander,
Pete Baston, and Judith Streit
January 22, 2019

# CHAPTER 1
# The Time of Your Life

*"In the time of your life, live – so that in that wondrous time you shall not add to the misery and sorrow of the world, but shall smile to the infinite delight and mystery of it."* William Saroyan[4]

When someone says "you will have the time of your life," it usually relates to a peak experience. However, the above quote contains a deeper meaning that refers to life as influenced by engagement with the economy. What are we living for? Is it only the money earned, the material things it will buy and the status we think it will deliver? Does the never-ending buying of new "stuff" and accumulation of more-and-more property really satisfy for long or deliver true happiness?

Thomas Jefferson would have answered, "No." He wrote that "the pursuit of happiness" was one of the inalienable rights of people, along with "life" and "liberty." Some thinking at the time would have substituted "property" for "happiness" but Benjamin Franklin supported Jefferson in downplaying "property," and "happiness" stayed in the Declaration of Independence. It is thought that in 1776 "happiness" may have meant "prosperity, thriving, wellbeing," broader in meaning than property.[5]

Contemporary research reinforces what was known in the 1700s: increases in income promote well-being up to a point, above which greater income is associated with less satisfaction.[6]

Under the current economic system, we are caught in a web that extracts our time and Earth's resources but keeps many of us tethered to dead-end jobs that pay too little. While these jobs do pay the bills, they often suck the joy out of life. We take the natural curiosity and creativity of children and move them through an educational system that, in most cases, remains grounded in a 19th-century model of preparing workers for industry. Too often, education values conformity and is more focused on preparation for a job than on seeking the type of knowledge that will help each person develop their talents and achieve their highest potential. In our working years we devote a high percentage of the time we have, the time of our lives, to engagement with the economic system. Certainly, this is fulfilling and time well spent for some, but for too many it is not truly rewarding—neither in terms of the time spent nor the money compensation for the work.

Looking deeply into the impact of the current Money-Centered Economy on our lives and the health of our planet, consider how we, as individuals and as a community, can promote a Life-Centered Economy that will better serve us, our children and grandchildren while preserving a viable ecosystem.

### *A Riddle for Our Times*

If the voice of advertising fell silent—what would people want?"

—Mike Nickerson[7]

How did we get here, embedded in a money-centered economy? A short history of American consumerism begins in the 1920s when business interests feared flagging consumer demand would stall the economy, and a major advertising effort was begun to link the universal wish for status, love and self-esteem with consumerism. With the Depression and then World War II combining to create pent-up consumer demand, the manufacturing sector transitioned from military products to consumer products, and a wave of post-war consumption was unleashed that continues to today. The advertising message succeeded, and now such things as the right cell phone, sneakers or vacation destination are considered necessities or are deemed to confer respect.

For many people, the message that more possessions bring happiness is a cruel joke since many of these are out of

Figure 1: The "Rat Race" by Polyp[8]

reach.[9] A whole range of human needs should be fairly met by the current economic system, but the never-ending quest to satisfy more "wants" is unsustainable. Many people who are exhausted by the long hours of work needed to afford ever more things are questioning their worth. Do all these things really bring happiness? (*Figure 1*)

### *Collateral Damage*

The consumer-based economy depends on planned obsolescence, so that new desirable products continue to replace the ones we have, which still are usually very functional, but nevertheless are consigned to waste—either downgraded by recycle or deposited in landfills. This wasteful process is dependent on the ever-increasing and unsustainable depletion of natural resources, many of which are non-renewable. And the conversion process of these resources to wastes is polluting the environment and thus degrading the ecosystem.

The current economy also promotes inequality, along with the irresponsible use of natural resources. World Bank economists have calculated that the wealthiest 10 percent of the world's population uses about 60 percent of the world's resources. If this 10 percent reduced their consumption to the average of the rest of humanity, total global resource use would be cut in half. Moreover, a 2015 report by Oxfam found the wealthiest 10 percent were responsible for half of all greenhouse gas (GHG) emissions, but the poorest half of the world's people were only responsible for about 10 percent of GHG.[10] Reducing consumption by the wealthiest would not only reduce GHG emissions but also allow improvements in others' standard of living.

Besides depriving future generations of adequate natural resources and a viable ecosystem, the current economy also deprives them of human resources. David Leonhardt's column, "Lost Einsteins: Innovations We're Missing" described the Equality of Opportunity Project, which correlates monetary wealth with the likelihood of becoming an inventor. The researchers linked tax records with patent records for the most highly cited and significant patents. They then linked these records with elementary school test scores for some patent-holders.[11]

Math scores were found to be a good predictor of the likelihood of an invention, but low-income students who scored in the top five percent of third graders were no more likely to become inventors than below-average scorers from affluent families. Middle-class innovation rates were closer to those of the poor than those of the affluent. The gaps are large: 6.5 out of 1000 upper-income students who excelled at math eventually got a patent, but for low-income students who also excelled at math, the number was only 1.2. According to this study, we appear to be missing out on most inventors from among the poor, middle class, women, African Americans and Southerners.[12]

## *The Current Economic Lens*

Inherent in the current economic system are the assumptions that people are only self-interested, have infinite wants and will continually seek to satisfy them, that moral values are irrational, and that concerns for other living beings can be disregarded. The current economic lens is based on the corporate requirement to maximize profits for shareholders, with other stakeholders left wanting.

The present economic system fosters inequality, which is not only immoral in itself, but also causes a whole range of social harms.[13] The ever-widening gap between earned and unearned incomes, where too much of net sales receipts goes to shareholders, leaves workers without enough income to buy the goods and services they produce. Inequality leads to insecurity, societal tension and moral regression as individuals vie for self-preservation.[14] A pervasive lack of felt safety and felt belonging as a respected member of a caring community is a driver of social tension and violent regression. Warning signs are flashing—society is on a dystopic path.[15] The key triggers for social regression are evident in news stories every day: (1) fear for safety; (2) loss of security (not knowing where the next meal or support for elderly survival is coming from); (3) loss of community (experiencing discrimination); (4) loss of agency (inability to live the life aspired to). These are pressures for social regression.[16]

A truly rational analysis would show that dependence on unending economic growth is unsustainable with finite planetary boundaries. A more realistic view is given in Kate Raworth's book, *Doughnut Economics*, where she proposes a 21st century compass (*Figure 2, p. 6*).[17] This depicts a foundational inner circle that shows the basic needs of human society, a band of sustainable existence for both humans and the planet, and an ecological ceiling band that needs to be preserved. The inner social foundation ring consists of 12 basic categories of human needs, such as food, health, education, etc. The outer ring represents nine essential ecological boundaries determined by an international group of earth scientists, such as carbon dioxide in the atmosphere. According to data available by their 2017 publication date, there were major shortfalls in the social foundation for health, social equity and representative governance while there was an overshoot of the ecological ceiling for sustainable

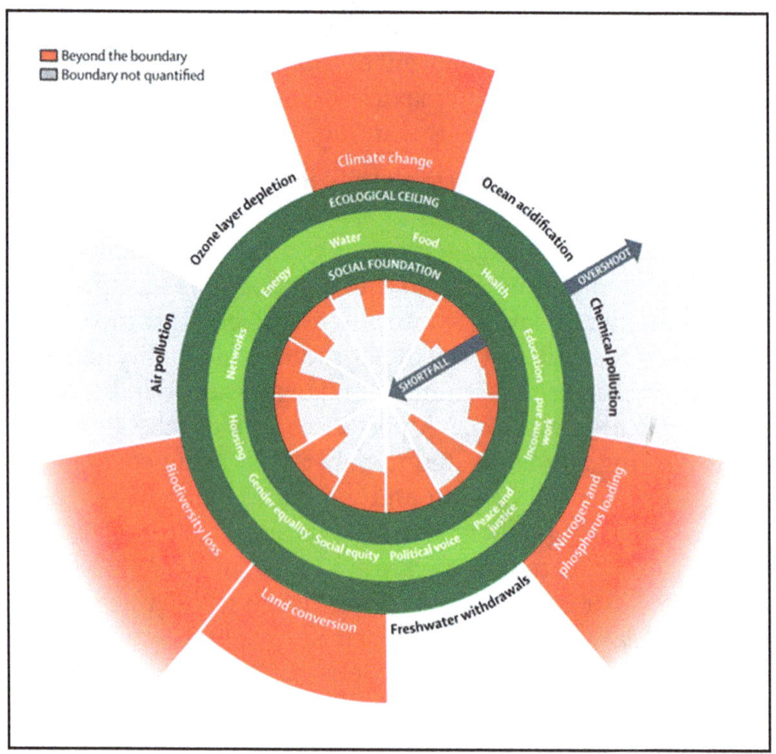


Figure 2: Raworth, 2017. "Doughnut Economy"[18]

atmospheric carbon dioxide, nitrogen/phosphorus fertilizer application, deforestation and biodiversity loss.[19]

Perhaps the worst feature of the current economy is the practice of discounting the future, and thereby shortchanging our children and generations to come. The discounting concept assumes that the present monetary value of a resource is greater than its future value, to the extent that the net interest rate is higher than the inflation rate. Discounting too highly leads to the dubious conclusion that saving natural resources for the future is uneconomic.

For example, $100 not invested today at five percent interest would only be worth $95 in a year, and within 25 years would have lost about 2/3 of its value. So applying this "failure to invest" to the extraction of natural resources, $1,000,000 worth of trees or oil today would be worth less than

$7,000 in 100 years. But if the forest is cut down today and sold, with the money invested at five percent, the monetary value would be assumed to multiply 130 times in 100 years.[20]

### *When Is It Rational to Kill the Goose that Lays the Golden Egg?*

Folk wisdom would say never kill it, but the discounting concept says kill it under certain circumstances. The goose owner has two choices: Keep the goose and sell golden eggs in perpetuity or kill the goose and sell it to get money that can earn interest in perpetuity. Current economics would say to take whichever yields the most money, but monetization doesn't take into account the total impact of losing the "golden eggs"—such as wiping out a forest ecosystem or an ocean fishery.[21]

## *An Alternative Moral Lens*

The economic lens, under which our society operates, is not a natural law—it has been constructed by humans and it can be changed by humans. Our history of civilization has twin strands of cooperation and competition, and our current system emphasizes the latter. In his 2018 column on altruism, David Brooks made the point that monetizing a voluntary action has a stultifying effect on the process and leads to a diminished outcome. Our institutions that support a moral lens, such as churches, guilds, and community organizations have been to some degree supplanted by those that feature an economic lens—the market and the state. We need to rebuild institutions that foster our natural tendency to cooperate with one another.[22]

A good move in this direction would be to replace the Gross Domestic Product (GDP) as a measure of economic activity with a more meaningful index, such as the Genuine Progress Indicator (GPI). The GDP captures some economic activity, whether good or bad, and also misses a lot. Digging a strip mine would be counted in GDP, but not any resulting pollution. But grow vegetables in your garden and share with others, and it does not get counted at all. The GPI instead focuses on overall wellbeing by subtracting out bad things like the cost of crime and declining water quality and adds in things such as volunteer work that GDP does not count. Until 1979 both GDP and GPI increased in the US, but then GDP continued to grow while GPI stalled. This has been attributed to income inequality and social/environmental costs rising faster than consumption-related benefits.

Two states, Maryland and Vermont, were leaders in adopting GPI and 20 states discussed it at a summit for "GPI in the States." There are also some similar measures in use internationally, such as the Human Development Index (HDI), Gross National Income (GNI) and the Inclusive Wealth Index (IWI).[23]

## *Beyond Wellbeing: Satisfaction and Meaning*

But what if the true measure of economic wellbeing is not truly quantifiable even by more sophisticated measuring sticks? Perhaps it depends more on our role as a participant. With the rise of Artificial Intelligence (AI) and robotics, there has been a great deal of speculation on how the workplace of the future will evolve. Robert C. Wolcott raises the questions of how society would adapt to a reduced need for human work. If such a development occurred, it would be important to reduce the inequality of wealth. History shows that extreme inequality has been dealt with either through politics or violence or both. He draws heavily on a book by Hannah Arendt, *The Human Condition*, in which she makes a distinction among Labor, for metabolic necessities like food, Work that creates artifacts and infrastructures that outlast us, like houses and works of art, and finally Action—how we interact with other human beings in the public sphere. As AI and robotics increasingly perform labor and work, more of us will have time to ascend to the realm of action. Some people may still choose to engage in labor or work, but the key distinction is choice. Our grandchildren may be able to

***A Waiter***

Robert (not his real name) was a waiter we knew, now retired, who was memorable. He was enthusiastic in describing various dishes, and would suggest the best level of seasoning as well as when portions were large enough to share. Over time we exchanged some personal information, such as fondness for cats, but he was never intrusive. At one point we complimented him on his consistent helpfulness, and he said "I love what I do." —John Lodenkamper

***A Teacher***

Our son's third grade teacher was truly masterful in unleashing the curiosity and creativity of her students. During parent visits we observed small groups of pupils and individuals working simultaneously on a variety of projects and assignments. Although bordering on pandemonium, there was palpable joy in the atmosphere and a whole lot of learning was going on! —John Lodenkamper

pursue a life of engagement and exploration or of gardening and cooking if that is their choice.[24]

If one is fortunate in today's economic system, it is possible to engage in a fulfilling occupation but it is all too rare. One can certainly follow one's genius in all walks of life, as noted in the side bars on a waiter and a teacher. Some jobs in the technical or management sectors would seem to offer greater opportunity for self-fulfillment, but it is likely that a great many of those so employed, when looking back over their careers would find precious few periods of time that they truly enjoyed. Joy is the key—when we travel in the right direction with our lives, we know it through increasing joy.

Satisfaction from our engagement with the economy really flows from our "doing" rather than our "consuming." Studies have shown that our happiness arises from our contributions that win the respect of our peers rather than more stuff or greater wealth. If we are diligent in seeking that place where our talents and our values intersect, then we will find our vocation as Aristotle advised over 2500 years ago. When we challenge ourselves to approach our careers with a mindset of exploration and experimentation, we can open the way to a fulfilling life-course.[25]

In envisioning a "Joyful Economy," James Gustav Speth ends that section of his essay with excerpts from a much earlier essay by John Maynard Keynes:

> *"For the first time since his creation man will be faced with his real, his permanent problem – how to use his freedom from pressing economic cares, how to occupy [his] leisure… how to live wisely and agreeably and well…*
>
> *"When the accumulation of wealth is no longer of high social importance, there will be great changes in the code of morals. The love of money as a possession …will be recognized for what it is, a somewhat disgusting morbidity, one of those semi-criminal, semi-pathological propensities which one hands over with a shudder to the specialists…*
>
> *"I see us free, therefore, to return to some of the most sure and certain principles of religion and traditional virtue – that avarice is a vice, that the exaction of usury is a misdemeanour, and the love of money is detestable, that those walk most truly in the paths of virtue and sane wisdom who take least thought for the morrow. We shall once more value ends above means and prefer the good to the useful. We shall honour those who can teach us how to pluck the hour and the day virtuously and well, the delightful people who are capable of taking direct enjoyment in things….*
>
> *"Chiefly, do not let us overestimate the importance of the economic problem, or sacrifice to its supposed necessities other matters of greater and more permanent significance."*[26]

In the broader sense, the "Time of Your Life" covers your lifespan. This raises the questions, "what are you living for?" and "how are you going about it?" You can look back on your past and decide to change your course in the future. And then, at the end of your life, your memorials truly will be celebrations.

## Memorials: Celebration of a Life

Memorials generally get right at the things that really matter in life. Memorial gatherings to celebrate the life of a person who has died usually feature touching remembrances of relationships—with family, friends, neighbors, colleagues and others in the person's circles of community. These poignant messages often relate the time that the deceased spent on one or many occasions within the relationships.

The typical comments below for "Don's" (not a real person) memorial are an amalgamation from many memorial events. Don was a husband, father, grandfather, and friend to many in his communities of interest for both work and leisure.

- His son remembered the time and patience he had taken to teach him fly-fishing, leaving him with a life-long appreciation of nature.
- A colleague spoke of how giving Don was in substituting for his classes when he had travel conflicts.
- His daughter related a conversation during a day's ride to check out a college, wherein he had bolstered her confidence to choose a challenging major subject.

Figure 3. You don't see many tombstones like this.

- Don was an avid gardener and even experimented with more nutritious heirloom vegetables. A fellow enthusiast recalled Don taking the time to show him the intricacies of this approach.
- His wife spoke tearfully of his embracing their marriage as a full partnership, and taking time to discuss her concerns through their many years together. She also spoke of how their two dogs were such a comfort to him during his final illness.
- A former student of his had been stimulated to pursue an international career, and now was based in South America, due to extra time that Don had spent outside of class in a counseling role.
- One member of his faith community recalled that Don was always willing to spend the extra time on committee work necessary to reach a satisfactory conclusion.
- His granddaughter spoke of the quality time they spent together when she introduced him to social media.

Mention is rarely, if ever, made of all the material things that the person possessed. We do not hear about size of house, type of car, list of "toys" or dollar value of the estate.

How ironic that our human society has evolved such that the vast majority spend their precious time on Earth in the pursuit of material goods, rather than the things that really matter—that are worth remembering about a person. Some spend their time simply meeting basic necessities because society's income distribution is so skewed. These material pursuits have greatly expanded since World War II with the introduction of TV advertising. Earth's natural resources are being consumed—the fossil fuels, metals, forests and fisheries. Within a very few generations little will be left for future generations. Instead we are leaving them the legacy of a plundered, toxic planet while we spend our lifetimes on material pursuits instead of the things that really matter.

# CHAPTER 2
# Our Economic System Reimagined

## The Money-Centered Economy

The underlying assumption of the current Money-Centered Economic System is that the economy is the overarching reason for being, with the human social system subservient to it and the ecosystem at the bottom of the hierarchy to be exploited for money regardless of consequences. The Money-Centered Economic System operates on the premise of continued economic growth, but that growth is based on consumption of non-renewable resources and overexploitation of many renewable resources. As a result of valuing money over life the Money-Centered Economic System is destroying the ecosystem and also diminishing the quality of our human lives.

The Money-Centered Economic System is both unsustainable for Earth and exploitive of the vast majority of the humans it should serve. The metrics that govern it, such as Gross Domestic Product (GDP), take no account of the natural capital that it transforms into an excessive accumulation of "stuff" nor of the planet-killing pollution that results. Surely no one claims that resources stored in Earth's crust are inexhaustible, so the question of peak production followed by decline due to unavailability is not a question of "if" but of "when."

Figure 4 (*p.14*) shows the results of a comprehensive 2012 BBC estimate of remaining non-renewable resources.This illustrates very dramatically some serious problems if we continue with "business as usual" in our Money-Centered Economy. Indium, which is used in touchscreens and solar

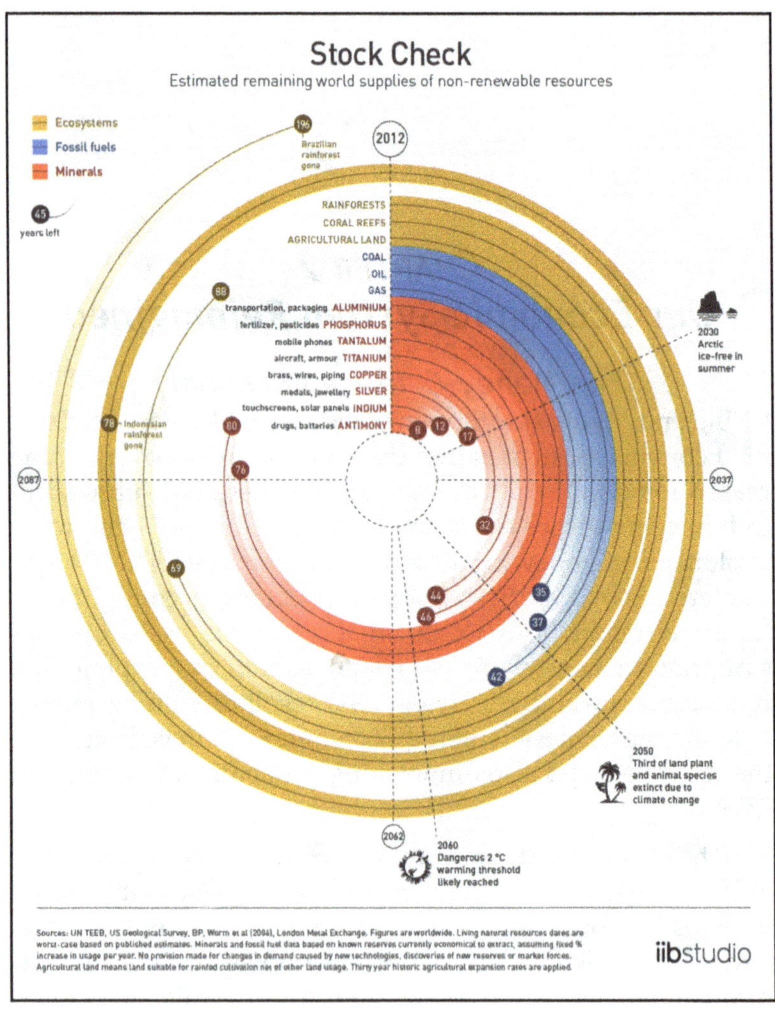


Figure 4: Natural Resource Inventory.[27]

panels, would be used up in 12 years; copper in 32 years; oil in 37 years; and coral reefs would be gone in 88 years. How can the Money-Centered Economy's built-in mandate for resource-based growth continue indefinitely?

It is true that lower grade mineral ores and fossil fuel deposits can still be found in order to delay the onset of resource exhaustion. However, the lower the grade of the resource, the more energy is required to extract it; a greater amount of waste material comes with it to be disposed of into the environment. Ecological economics has risen up to try and deal with these problems, but it has focused mostly on monetizing the environmental externalities. David Korten reminds us to be cautious with this approach. He relates his meeting with some indigenous leaders prior to the Rio+20 International Conference:

> *"These leaders observed that in preparatory meetings, Wall Street interests had argued that to save nature we must value her by pricing her. It seems a sensible argument – but the indigenous leaders pointed out a familiar pattern: First price, then privatize, then commodify, then securitize, and then profit from a new round of speculative financial games."*[28]

This state of affairs has also engendered a major global imbalance in the consumption of resources, wherein the US with less than five percent of world population consumes roughly 25 percent of the natural resources.[29] This leads to an impossible dilemma as developing countries try to emulate the well-communicated lifestyle of the US. Obviously, the resources are not available for a worldwide US lifestyle, but since the US is the current model in many places, should not the US lead the way to a better alternative?

In the course of spreading this Money-Centered Economy globally, inequality of both income and wealth is increasing. In 2015 the 62 wealthiest people in the world had more total wealth than the least-wealthy 50 percent of the world's population.[30] International corporations have become more powerful than many governments. Workers are increasingly marginalized into part-time or dead-end jobs just to keep ever decreasing healthcare and pension benefits. This system has lifted average corporate CEO compensation in the US to greater than 276 times that of the average employee.[31] This CEO compensation has come to represent a mark of value in an economic "game." But is a CEO 276 times better as a human being? As a spouse, parent, friend or co-worker? On reflection, most of us would say "no," probably including some of those CEOs.

Figure 5: Money-Centered "Pyramid"[32]

These excesses of the Money-Centered Economy are driven by consumer demand for more and more of the latest attractive products fueled by advertising. Many embrace escapism via buying the next "cool" thing and immersion in the pervasive entertainment options that are available. For those who through a combination of luck and skill are able to thrive in the current system, it can be luxury goods like private jets for those at the top of the pyramid and an excess of living space, clothes, gadgets and "toys" for those further down. Although the Money-Centered Economic System has provided better basic living conditions globally for many, it has turned malignant and is extracting more and more wealth from everyone only to benefit those at the top and is leaving an increasingly large base of poverty at the bottom (*Figure 5*).

In the course of providing a measure of material well-being it has had negative impacts on true well-being. It has disrupted families and communities through geographical dislocation in pursuit of jobs. It has polluted the habitat of both humans and the other life-forms that share Earth. It has sentenced the vast majority of the workforce to unfulfilling jobs and increasing time pressure.

***The credo of the Money-Centered Economy is "Time is Money."***

## The Life-Centered Economy

A Life-Centered Economy would nourish life, the lives of all people and the beings with whom we share Earth. In a Life-Centered Economy our individual lives—our time on Earth between birth and death—and our relationship to the communities in which we live would be valued. Also valued would be our connections with family, friends and co-workers, and also the wider community of our networks with houses of worship, civic organizations and special interest groups, including the growing virtual community via social media. In the Life-Centered Economy, the plant and animal life on Earth, and on which all human life depends would be highly valued.

The word "economics" derives from the Greek words for household management. In the Life-Centered Economy attention would be re-focused on our families and households, our friends and neighbors in the larger community. The true values in life would be supported by how we spend our time. The larger household of the Earth would be honored. Insofar as we manage portions of it, we would do so sustainably so that we endow our children with a livable legacy. Our knowledge of science increasingly supports indigenous beliefs that we are connected in a community with all of nature. We know that the only new thing coming into our home on Earth is sunlight, and through its role in photosynthesis, sunlight supports all plant and animal life-forms. Earth's crust is a treasure chest of resources, many of which have already been taken out and used. That remaining must be used more mindfully so that some are left for future generations. Those resources must be consumed in a much more responsible manner so as not to irrevocably pollute Earth's ecosystems.

A viable economic system in today's world would provide for basic human needs such as clean air, clean water, sanitation, nourishing food, shelter and energy for cooking and temperature control, clothing, transportation, access to electronic communications, adequate healthcare and relevant life-long education to develop our talents. It also would be structured for meaningful occupations that permit all capable adults to pursue paths to realize their individual potential. Compensation for work would cover basic needs during one's working life and retirement years, and there would be adequate time outside of work to enjoy leisure with family, friends, community or by oneself. In order to achieve these goals sustainably, the economic system would need to be re-localized to the extent practicable. This would entail the development of economic communities that are self-sufficient for many of the basic needs.

At the dawn of the industrial revolution, individual craftsmanship and entrepreneurship were more prevalent than at present, and it was not so necessary for someone to "give you a job." Today we see there are already corporate efforts to promote free-lance knowledge workers that are hired on a project-by-project basis via the Internet for their specialized contributions. Likewise, the incipient "sharing" economy relies on the Internet for connections and transactions. It should be possible for worker co-operatives to utilize these platforms as well, and to get out from under corporate control. Earlier "revolutions" with economic aspects (slavery, feudalism, etc.) amounted to merely changing one set of exploitive masters for another with the new masters still keeping the economic surplus for themselves. A present-day antidote would be to greatly expand worker-owned cooperatives.[33]

Economic activity would be scaled to the smallest units that are possible for overall efficiency, including transportation from outside the community economic unit. Agriculture and light manufacturing would be located near the point of consumption or use. The advent of 3D printing permits local light manufacturing of a range of tools and parts. More complex and heavier manufacturing that is not amenable to local scaling could be geared towards product reuse and recycle rather than planned obsolescence, with capability for local repair. There are already trends in this direction.

Individuals might be increasingly educated via online open source courses, and taught skills intergenerationally by family and community. With adequate income for all, work could become more decentralized with some time spent gardening, on arts, crafts or online knowledge-based projects. There would be less time spent commuting and reporting up hierarchal chains of command, and more time spent with family, friends, neighbors, and larger circles of community. You could get your life back!

***The credo of the Life-Centered Economy is "Time is Life."***

## *The Economic Structure Reimagined: A Life-Centered Economy*

In a Life-Centered Economy, the economic system is a subset of the human social system which in turn is a subset of the ecological system. It calls us to practice ***economic synergism***—not capitalism or socialism. Economic synergism emphasizes the interconnectedness of all life. Synergism is the way the components of the Life-Centered Economy would work together for the greater good of all the stakeholders, expanding opportunites for all. The Life-Centered Economy works with nature and truly acknowledges the systemic aspect of the ecosystem. Cooperation between economic entities is employed for win-win rather than zero-sum outcomes. Individuals are encouraged to act in their "own interest," as Adam Smith advocated. But, in order for this "invisible hand" to bring forth the greatest good for society, as Smith envisioned, individuals must be interested in rising to their highest human potential in a community of valued relationships, not just in making as much money as possible.

How might such a Life-Centered Economy appear in practice? It would probably utilize some appropriate technology along with a revival of relevant traditional skills. A future community-based economic system would likely incorporate some "makers' districts" wherein large buildings are re-purposed as hubs for units of craft production, light manufacturing, food provision and various trades. There would be a mix of small proprietorships and worker co-ops, as well as a highly developed sharing community which improves on current auto and bike sharing systems, and perhaps utilizes libraries as loan centers for tools, etc. as has been implemented already. Urban agriculture, farmer's markets, and community gardens would be further expanded. An initiative was recently announced to provide micro grids for solar energy that could be a good fit for a community-based economic unit.

Much of the good work on economic reform suggests better government regulation of the established system, but this system is subject to political whim. Real reform is expected to come mainly from the bottom up rather than the top down. The key to this change is the underutilized potential for informed and massively connected consumer and citizen activism. It is true that in many respects our economic system is intertwined with government, as in taxation, trade law, etc., and it is beyond the scope of this initiative for a new economic system to address that connection more than peripherally except in key areas that can be influenced by grassroots action. In many cases there are already successful models in place, as in universal healthcare, which can be established through political action.

In the Life-Centered Economy, individual economic agency would be restored by embracing foundational values that underpin the basic economic functions.

The foundational values of a Life-Centered Economy foster time over money, quality over quantity, sustainability over depletion, human potential over exploitation, and small-scale over large-scale.

## Time over Money

A famous TV ad depicts people spending time with loved ones and nature as "priceless;" it then goes on to say "There are some things money cannot buy—for everything else there is MasterCard."

Money is needed in an economic system, but in the Money-Centered Economy it has become the master instead of the servant. The creation of money promotes unwarranted economic growth, and its manipulation by the financial sector produces nothing of real value, only such things as collateralized debt obligations (CDOs), which David Korten calls "phantom wealth."

Money also relates to future time because money is discounted in the future: A dollar today is deemed to be worth more than a dollar in the future due to its earning capacity. This is called the time value of money, a core principle of our current system. So we see an unhealthy focus on the short term to the detriment of the long term. By encouraging economic growth through faster consumption of resources and slower investment in environmental protection, the value of the needs of future generations are discounted as compared to the value of the needs of the present generation.

Geoff Mulgan's book, *The Locust and the Bee*, compares some aspects of the current system with a time-oriented system and speculates on the implications of the latter. It may encompass both meaningful human life cycles and longer cycles of ecological time. He notes that numbers in the current system are time-based, future-discounted, forecast and hedged—and asks how such mechanisms could be used in service of the quality of lived time.[34]

The authors of *Creating Wealth* point out that valuing the time of individuals in monetary terms can depend on their skills and knowledge, with a brain surgeon's time more valuable than that of street sweeper for example. But they note that even lower skill jobs, along with those that are not valued in monetary terms, are essential for our society. Paying even low wages for all the time spent each day on child care, elder care, and food preparation would bankrupt our current economic system.[35]

Time is a great equalizer, with everyone having the same 24 hours per day. The current economic system largely dictates how time is spent. It has been estimated that hunter-gatherers had a 20-30 hour work week and that this held during the Middle Age feudal system, with extra time spent in community and family interaction. The present system has diminished the extra time available, but there are still volunteer workers for firefighting, soup kitchens, thrift stores, and youth groups. Communities run on time and time is the glue that holds them together.

The Life-Centered Economy will need a monetary system as a means of exchange and storage of surplus, but not the current debt-creating system that drives unwarranted growth. Although the digital currency Bitcoin suffers from speculation and built-in deflationary aspects, it has spawned a wide array of alternative digital currency startups. Local currencies are on the rise, which mostly can be converted into national currencies. There are movements toward community banks, credit unions, and public banking in order to break the grip of "too big to fail" Wall Street banks. The time bank concept for exchanging hours of services could be further enhanced and expanded, and this would serve as an alternative means of compensation. In short, money would serve the Life-Centered Economy, it would not be the master.

## *Quality over Quantity*

Our current system is geared to growth, and it is overwhelmingly growth in the quantity of material things. It has given rise to an enormous array of consumer goods that are presented via sophisticated advertising as aspects of "the good life" but, as has been well documented, fail to satisfy once the newness wears off. Workers are motivated to earn ever more money to buy ever more stuff, to the point that garages can become filled with stuff rather than cars and the overflow fuels a thriving storage rental business. The folly of this system is captured by a recent bumper sticker that said: "He who dies with the most toys is still dead."

The famous quote from Emerson, "Things are in the saddle, and ride mankind,"[36] is even more meaningful now than in the 19th century. Our time is consumed by trying to deal with gadgetry on the latest upgrade, which most of us do not really need. Would it not be wiser and more satisfying to choose products that we can enjoy for many years? What if we sought quality of life instead of more material goods?

We may see another positive development that has surprisingly begun by excesses of the current system in saddling young people with a burden of student loan debt. Many of them already have left telephone land lines behind and operate solely with a cell phone. They are slow to buy cars and, in many cases, have no plans to do so. It may be the beginning of a backlash against the drive for "more stuff" that has been heavily promoted for so long, and partly created by difficulty in taking on further debt on top of the student loan balances. Embracing the sharing economy may slow production of housing and transportation as underutilized existing capacity is filled.

If we rethink our real material needs, we might realize that less work would be required to fill our real needs, leaving us freer from financial pressure and perhaps better positioned to choose a more satisfying occupation. Rather than conspicuous consumption, self-esteem should be based on how good we are. In our relationships with friends and family and our commercial dealings, we would have compassion towards those in less fortunate circumstances. Then the fulfillment of our highest potential and our legacy would be leaving Earth in better condition than we found it.

When we reflect on the truly important things in life, such as, love, beauty, wisdom and truth, we realize that they are not quantifiable and certainly not capable of being monetized!

## *Sustainability over Depletion*

Growth in the current system is ultimately based on consumption of natural resources, many of which are non-renewable and therefore unsustainable in the long run. The industrial revolution has been driven by the extraction of fossil fuels and mineral resources from Earth's crust. As material growth has burgeoned, more and more of these mineral resources have been used, to the point where shortages loom across the board from rare earth metals needed for high-tech electronic devices[37] to even sand, which is needed for concrete production[38] and many materials in between. But as consumers we can resist the temptation to buy the latest style and more and more "stuff" that we do not really need. Instead we should seek products designed with reusable components, sometimes called "cradle-to-cradle" or "circular economy design," in a shift to more sustainable production.

When sustainability-minded consumers demand durable goods, products that are repairable, rather than being designed for planned obsolescence, we can expect local repair shops to emerge. The toaster that lasted our parents a lifetime and now must be replaced every few years illustrates the planned obsolescence adopted by much of industry. This policy consumes unwarranted amounts of energy and material to produce shoddy products which then clog landfills. In *Cradle to Cradle*[39] the authors posit a world of abundance rather than limits, if we harness human creativity in sustainable product design so as to leave an ecological footprint we can be proud of. They note that ants have a total biomass greater than humans and have been busily producing for millions of years, but their activity has nourished plants, animals and soil. Environmental regulation can be seen as a sign of design failure, since it permits release of "acceptable" levels of contaminants. Products can be designed so that "waste" does not exist; it can be either biological or technological nutrients—feedstock for other processes.

## Human Potential over Exploitation

Just as the Money-Centered Economy has depended on irresponsible extraction of natural resources, it also routinely exploited the workforce from the very beginnings of the industrial revolution. Some of the most egregious practices of child labor, long workdays and unsafe working conditions have been eliminated through regulation (at least in more developed countries), but the worship of profit over life continues to oppress. A 2010 example was the deadly explosion in a West Virginia coal mine caused by management pushing production ahead of safety.[40]

Labor is now seen as a cost to be minimized, rather than a human resource. What if instead we designed work to engage the individual's potential and then shared benefits from the increased productivity? Two of W. Edwards Deming's 14 points for quality management are especially relevant here, for reclaiming "quality of life" in the workplace. They are driving out fear and removing barriers to pride of workmanship. The early development of the US economy included both a "can-do" mentality for individuals, who took pride in their ability to master a range of crafts, and a strong commitment to cooperation as in a community barn-raising effort. We need to reclaim these values as individuals engage as entrepreneurs in the gig and sharing economic sectors, and join in worker co-ops that counter corporate platforms which take a lion's share of the benefits and treat workers like interchangeable cogs in the system.[41]

## Small-scale over Large-scale

A Life-Centered Economy would have a natural bias toward the principle of subsidiarity, defined as operating on as small a scale as can be efficient and practical. Smaller economic units are closer to their stakeholders and to the ecosystem in which they operate and foster economic synergism. Smaller houses use less material to build and less energy to maintain. Re-localization is also a key element of the new system since it intrinsically minimizes energy for transportation. With the rise of community-supported agriculture and farmers' markets people have rediscovered that food grown closer to home tastes better.

Obviously, a locomotive factory has to be larger than a local tool and die maker, but it does not need to consolidate with other locomotive manufacturers that already have similar economies of scale. All too often, large mergers benefit no one but the shareholders and have a negative impact on other stakeholders. Jobs are lost and the remaining workforce is expected to work harder. Suppliers are bullied into concessions for fear of losing a major piece of business. Customers suffer with ever poorer service administered by layers of management far removed from the point of sale. Ideally all stakeholders should benefit.

## Practical Aspects

The basic functions of an economic system have to address what shall be produced; who will produce it and with what resources; and how the benefits will be distributed.

**Demand:** What and how many goods and services should be produced? Notwithstanding serious faults in the current money-centered economic system, the market mechanism is very effective in balancing supply and demand for a wide range of products. While it is true that sophisticated advertising drives a lot of the demand, educated consumers are having more and more of an impact as exemplified by the rise in availability of organic food, "green" products and recyclable packaging.

Consumer purchasing in the US approaches 70 percent of GDP. Demand for food, clothing, shelter, durable goods and communication access is mainly governed by our decisions as consumers. Communication items are especially important because they enable us to make a potentially big positive impact on product supply. The ubiquitous smartphone has more computing power than NASA had for the moon landing.

Smartphones can be a very effective tool in promoting sustainability. They can read both traditional product line barcodes and the newer Quick Response (QR) black and white square codes, which are expected to provide ever-increasing levels of product information in the future.[42]

In addition to more informed choices at the point of sale, there have been many successful petitions and boycotts in support of sustainable products and improved processing and working conditions that have been organized by consumer advocacy groups. We can expect the size and influence of consumer organizations to continue to grow, and there are already some like Consumers International[43] a federation of more than 240 advocacy groups, that have global impact. Green America[44] is a national one-stop shop focused on sustainability, to give just two of many examples.

**Supply:** How shall goods and services be produced? By whom and with what resources and technology?

We should begin by emphasizing re-localization to the extent of avoiding diminished efficiency. Already there is consumer sentiment toward patronizing local shops rather than big box retailers and to procuring food from farmers' markets and community-supported agriculture. With local food, there are significant savings in food wastage as well as in transportation energy. There is also growing acceptance of sharing services for autos, bicycles, and shelter through the likes of Lyft and Airbnb, and lending "libraries" for tools such as power drills have been initiated. A whole spectrum of sharing options is becoming available.[45]

As the current economy has shifted more and more traditional jobs overseas, young people may be forced into beginning their careers through what has been called a gig economy. This in effect makes people into individual entrepreneurs, where they work project-by-project both online and offline in a variety of endeavors. While the Internet-based gig economy offers flexibility and a new range of opportunities, the enabling online platforms have so far been dominated by large corporations that unfortunately offer few or no worker benefits and little employment security. Gig workers are beginning to wring concessions from large companies.[46] Co-operatives potentially provide more democratic alternatives.[47]

Now makers' districts have taken co-working facilities to new levels and these units can combine light manufacturing via assembly or 3-D printing with other economic activity. A US Department of Energy study of 3-D printing, also known as "additive manufacturing," showed that this process can reduce material needs and costs by up to 90 percent, and where competitive (in lower volume production) it can exhibit energy savings of 50 percent or more.[48] This process had increased by 26 percent in 2015 to be worth almost $5.2 billion in products and services, and is projected for a strong further increase to $550 billion by 2025.[49]

Habitat for Humanity was the top US homebuilder for private dwellings in 2015. This positive statistic supports the importance of local involvement in providing low-cost housing for low-income people.[50] There is also an incipient do-it-yourself movement using open source design to construct low-cost ecological-friendly houses in a short period of time, which relies on a local barn-raising effort for final assembly.[51]

Technological improvements can be very helpful in mooring the economy to a sustainable system, but they are not likely to accomplish sustainability by themselves, as many hope they will. For one thing, they all require some energy and materials to function, lessening their total positive impact. It would be well for developed countries to seriously consider some of the appropriate small-scale technology that has been invented for the developing world. Simplicity is the key to many of these technologies. Wherever they are put to use, material and energy consumption is reduced.

**Benefits:** For whom shall goods and services be produced? Who will enjoy the benefits and how will they be distributed?

In order to honor the labor of the workforce, there needs to be a major realignment of the value of human capital versus financial capital, especially for large companies. There has been some movement to distribute corporate benefits among all stakeholders—labor, capital, management, suppliers, customers, community—not just shareholders alone. The environment also deserves a seat at the "stakeholder round table." (*Figure 6*) This trend needs to be reinforced through more boycotts, petitions, investor awareness and other forms of consumer activism.

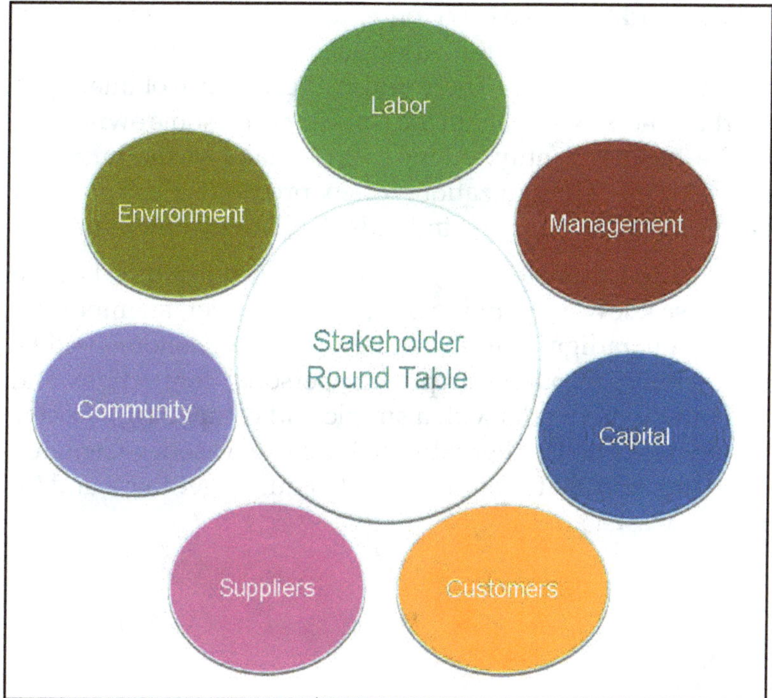


Figure 6: Cooperation Concept

With the vast knowledge available through the Internet, and the increasing impact of consumer organizations, it is possible to envision a movement to reverse the extreme inequity in much of the large corporate wage structure. What if petitions and boycotts were unleashed against irresponsible executive compensation?

In the case of a new technology start-up, there may be an entrepreneur with a really good idea, an initial management team with the skills to carry it forward, and a venture capitalist who could fund it. The Golden Rule of business is "he who has the gold rules," so the venture capitalist has the strongest position. Why is that, since all three components are needed? Part of the answer is that the capital is often invested from a distance while the other components are localized. There needs to be a rebalancing, perhaps through crowd-funding mechanisms, so that all stakeholders benefit equitably.

Nevertheless, we are seeing some areas of improvement for the workforce. To carry on with the technology sector, it is often the case that the workforce is compensated in part with stock ownership. There is also a resurgence of interest in worker co-ops where again the workforce has some ownership in the business entity. Along with a stake in the business, these types of organizations often promote a culture that encourages and supports individual creativity and initiative.

We are fortunate in having the Internet as a tool, both to dispense knowledge and to organize. However, an important key to a paradigm shift for a Life-Centered Economy will be to reach out through our present personal connections and community networks with a simple and compelling message that there is a better alternative to the current Money-Centered Economy and that there is a viable path to get there and no time to waste!

## *Transition to the Life-Centered Economy*

So how do we shift from the Money-Centered Economy, which seems so pervasive and powerful, to a Life-Centered Economy?

This initiative is grounded on the following premises:

- The shift to a new system cannot be seen as a negative; but rather as the positive ideal of "Quality of Life" replacing "Quantity of Stuff."
- Parents want to leave their children the legacy of a good future.
- A major grassroots effort will be required to a) focus consumer action on sustainability and b) establish cooperative platforms in the burgeoning gig and sharing economic sectors.

This discussion is focused on economic systems, and will leave aside questions of government systems which too often have been invoked as solutions to the current dysfunctional economy via rules and taxes. This paradigm shift may be aided by governance considerations, but is very unlikely to be initiated by today's "establishment" since its members benefit from the current system. There also would undoubtedly be a period where the Life-Centered Economy exists in parallel with a declining Money-Centered Economy, but the more deleterious aspects of the latter can be expected to undergo Schumpeter's "creative destruction" as they are overcome by sustainable demand trends.[52]

Such a significant change to a life-empowering system will need to be a grass-roots movement, and the opportunity is at hand along with the tools to seize it. It will involve a two-pronged approach, to both better-educate and better-organize the consumer and worker base of today's Money-Centered Economy pyramid. The current economy of unlimited growth via material consumption strongly depends on consumer demand. Re-shaping consumer demand towards sustainable products and against corporate greed could move the system in the right direction at a fundamental level. This market system is very efficient in responding to shifts in demand, such as we have seen for the availability of organic and gluten-free food and for non-GMO labeled products. We have already seen an impact from consumer boycotts, petitions and dissemination of consumer information via the Internet, but so far this has been rather loosely organized and just scratches the surface of what might be done.

Consumer and worker education will be directed toward:

1) valuing quality time in life over the quantity of things that money can buy and
2) raising consciousness about our connectedness to nature and the need to stop its destruction through material-based growth. It will also include stronger emphasis on the key skills needed to thrive in the gig economy and in re-localized economic functions, rather than the current fixation on college degrees.

Consumer and worker organization will take advantage of the market efficiency of the current system in responding to consumer demand, and focus a tidal wave of consumer action in favor of sustainable products. It will also act to connect workers to cooperative enterprises both on the Internet and in local communities.

Already there are some positive trends that can move us toward a Life-Centered Economy and should encourage us onward. Several of these are listed below:

**GMO labeling:** A pertinent illustration of consumer impact is the case of GMO labeling. GMO-using producers have been strongly resisting GMO labeling but this has given rise to Non-GMO labeling by their competition who do not use GMO, undercutting Big Agriculture resistance to GMO labeling. There has still been consumer pressure for GMO labeling but there was GMO industry-sponsored legislation which has recently become law that would allow GMO labeling only via barcodes or website access. This may well turn out to have unintended consequences for industry, as consumers are encouraged to use their powerful smartphone tool. A transparency revolution might be launched for food processing as well as ingredients. Companies that are doing the "right thing" may seize the chance to note this on their product codes and thereby benefit.[53]

**Healthy food/climate change connection:** The article cited below references a Gallup Poll showing that 45 percent of American consumers seek out organic food. Connecting to nature via local produce and concern over healthy food today can give rise to efforts that ensure healthy food for grandchildren tomorrow and thereby support a viable future for our planet. "This synergy between self-interest and altruistic motivation has only begun to be tapped." People-powered support of restorative agriculture can have a significant impact on combating climate change.[54]

**Smartphone tool:** This portable personal computer is seen as the defining technology of the age. It will play a fundamental role in the Internet of Things, which can improve household energy efficiency among many other applications. It will also be an enabler for the growing field of telemedicine via sending both pictures and data to a remote doctor. It is widely utilized in various financial transactions. Moreover, it has already been employed in large-scale political protests.[55]

**Blockchain technology:** Notwithstanding its usage for Bitcoin and possible application for other digital currencies, the underlying technology has gained wide interest.[56] It is still embryonic, but has been posed for "smart contracts" and decentralized ownership of digital platform co-operatives.

**Standards and labeling:** There is a growing movement for businesses to organize as a Benefit Corporation and/or become certified as a B Corp. Both have the same thrust, that of adhering to social and environmental standards, along with the pursuit of profits.[57]

Besides well-established social/environmental screens for mutual funds, there is now a Sustainability Accounting Standards Board that supports investor demand for better transparency of non-compliance risks. It is privately run, so not subject to political meddling, and is expected to continue to expand its reach due to customer demand.[58]

**Rustbelt to "brainbelt"**: In *The Smartest Places on Earth* the authors have identified many areas in both the US and Europe where declining centers of traditional manufacturing have become resurgent via smart manufacturing and connections with local institutions such as universities, research institutes and hospitals. They note that smart manufacturing relies on robotics, 3-D printing and the Internet of Things, and that workers need Science, Technology, Engineering and Math (STEM) skills more so than four-year college degrees. For each urban high-tech job, five additional jobs are created outside the tech sector—three professional and two non-professional. Finally, they say that the economic organizing principle should not be money, but the sharing of brainpower to address the Internet of Things. "The opportunity then is to base our activities around what best realizes our potential as human beings and as a society, not what puts more money in our pockets and portfolios."[59]

**FCC action on net neutrality:** Millions of citizen/ consumer messages to the Federal Communications Commission helped defeat an industry effort that would have favored certain large consumers with preferential bandwith. This regulation may be at risk for being revoked, but this is the type of single-issue political action that lends itself to a massive grassroots involvement. It is certainly critical to preserve the Internet as an organizing and knowledge tool for the whole range of consumer and citizen activism.

**Pipeline protests:** Grassroots protests against the Keystone XL pipeline and more recently the Standing Rock pipeline encroachment have both been successful, at least temporarily. Despite approvals by the Trump administration, these projects may not be completed. Of particular interest in the case of Standing Rock is an effective effort for divestment from the banks that are financing the project.

**Grassroots organizing:** Here is just a small sampling of some groups engaged in grassroots orgranizing—Grassroots Economic Organizing,[60] Seeds of a Good Anthropocene,[61] and Local Futures.[62]

Besides the examples of consumer action noted in the foregoing, the Spring 2015 issue of *Green American* lists the following accomplishments in the editorial "The Power is In Your Hands"

> *"In my 30-plus years as a green-economy advocate, every major change that I've witnessed began with demand. For example, what do Home Depot, Nike, Starkist, Dell, Apple, Hershey, General Mills and General Motors have in common?*
>
> *"They've begun to make significant change because, together, you and I, demanded sustainable lumber, sweatshop-free sneakers, dolphin-safe tuna, responsibly recycled computers and smartphones without poisoning workers, chocolate minus child labor, GMOs out of Cheerios and a wide selection of hybrids and electric cars.*
>
> *"And when we come together to amplify our voices and economic choices, change can happen rapidly."*[63]

## *Call to Action*

The seeds and sprouts of a new economic synergism are beginning to emerge and grow, as shown by the information presented above. It is most encouraging to see a multitude of progressive organizations working both locally and globally to move away from the current Money-Centered Economy.

However, to succeed in this crucial endeavor there are still some very important missing pieces:

1) There needs to be a powerful effort to connect these disparate groups in support of a common theme for a new story or paradigm, whether it be a Life-Centered Economy or something else. Whatever it is, it should have a ***positive*** message as in "quality of life," which was suggested here, in order to replace "quantity of stuff."
2) To accomplish the first task, there should be an appeal to "common sense" in order to reach "common ground." Grassroots organizing based on an appealing theme can cut through the prevalence of misinformation and fake news that could derail more unfocused activism.
3) This effort should also be informed by the successful campaign against tobacco smoking, which reportedly relied on generating some guilt, but not overwhelming

guilt that could simply be rationalized away. In this case it might be possible to center the message on leaving a viable legacy for our children, and invoking the Precautionary Principle to foster future sustainability.

4) To restore our agency as consumers: A concerted initiative should be launched to encourage a) informative product labeling by responsible businesses and b) consumer knowledge and action to favor such products.

5) To restore our agency as workers: Here the effort should be to promote worker co-ops for digital platforms addressing the gig economy, along with publicizing online and local community college education for critical skills.

The desired outcome of the steps above would be to focus massive consumer/citizen power on sustainable products, processes and businesses. The market system would then work to enhance the good and discard the bad.

Our tools are available via smartphones and the Internet—we all just need to connect!!

# CHAPTER 3
# Synergism in the Life-Centered Economy

## A Reevaluation

The Money-Centered Economy is driven to produce endless growth, but depends on limited non-renewable natural resources to do so—how can this be? It values the short term over the long term, and is thereby disposed to leave environmental damage for our children to fix, if they still can. It encourages us to value ourselves by the money and material possessions that we accumulate, leading us to seek more and more, rather than valuing ourselves by the quality time we spend as we develop our potential and meaningful personal relationships.

So how can this be changed to a Life-Centered Economy that honors all life on Earth? We have the Earth, with its limited mineral resources, and solar energy to support all plant and animal life, including human life. The Sun is the only replenishing input the Earth has. To change direction from a planet-destroying economy that is leading to extreme material inequality, we need to generate economic synergism, where the components of the socioeconomic system work together for the greater good in a way that makes the whole greater than the sum of the parts. The concept of economic synergism is depicted in Figure 7 (*p.38*).

Relationships among stakeholders would be mutually supporting—the system would be characterized by symbiosis. The parts support the whole and the whole supports the parts. Their interdependence is critical.

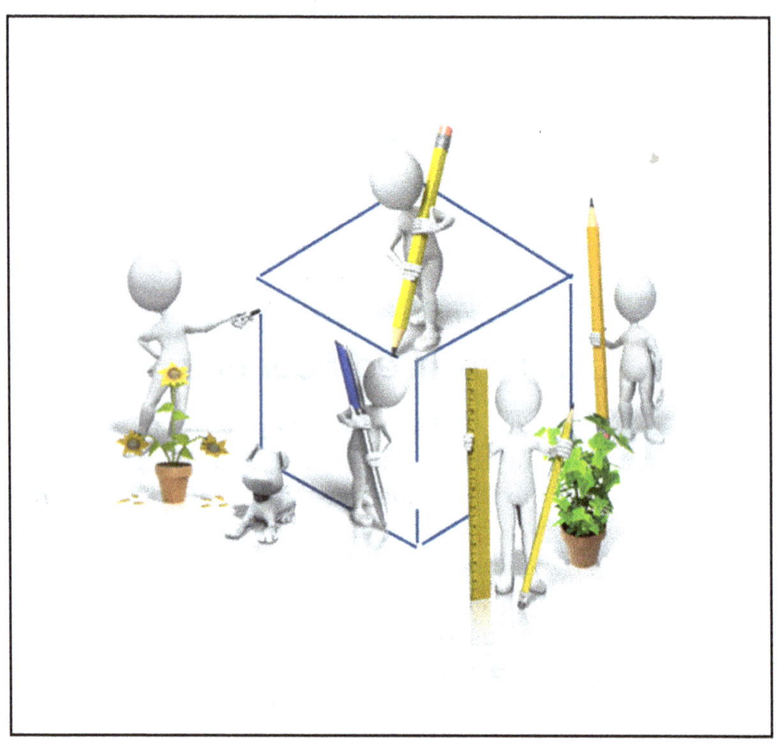

Figure 7: Synergism Concept

A concrete example of economic synergism can be found with local hardware stores, some of which are thriving despite competition from big box stores. The good ones have knowledgeable employees who exchange knowledge with customers. Customers bring in new problems and employees suggest new solutions—both are wiser. Some stores offer basic repair and maintenance services so that tools are not thrown away, but re-fitted for more years of use. By featuring knowledge of "green" products, these stores benefit the ecosystem. They provide opportunities for connections between customers from the surrounding community and the overall good will generated by word of mouth benefits the business.

In a Life-Centered Economy, humans are seen as stakeholders in all our various roles: producer, consumer, investor, and neighbor. Mother Nature, the provider of all our resources, is the ultimate stakeholder. We should think of her as our banker. Since the industrial revolution, the Money-Centered Economy has overdrawn Earth's resources in a way that weakens its ability to support life and "repaid" with overwhelming and damaging pollution instead of stewardship. In order to change this negative relationship, a key but underutilized resource can be mobilized—human potential. For this resource to be enabled, our central valuations must change from exploitation to stewardship with time and quality placed above money and quantity.

For the most part we now channel the natural curiosity of children towards measurable test results in school, and do not instill the critical thinking skills needed to discern the truth when bombarded by advertising and political propaganda. Higher education generally focuses more on training for an occupation than fostering creativity. On graduation most individuals end up in rather mundane jobs that do not fully utilize their capabilities. There are still some very engaging and interesting jobs, but these are not plentiful. Moreover, the current trend in the US is reducing or downgrading even mundane jobs via global outsourcing and automation. A real wealth of human potential is underutilized by our current economic system.

However, this untapped human potential can be the "missing ingredient" in a synergistic economic system that promotes a fair exchange among the human stakeholders while preserving key elements of the larger ecosystem that supports all life on Earth. We can begin to work "smarter, not harder" and refocus our lives on the time we spend rather than the money we accumulate. It is worth emphasizing: money can be accumulated but time cannot—a lifetime is a lifetime—so we should spend our time wisely as we live out our lives.

## *The Human Household*

The basic element in a synergistic economic system is the management of the human household, which was also the ancient Greek focus at the dawn of economic concepts. We can use this as a lens to examine the stimulation of synergistic aspects for the various system components. In his excellent book, *Building a Healthy Economy from the Bottom Up*, Anthony Flaccavento considers the role of households and their communities as foundational in the transition from "consumptive dependence to productive resilience." He notes the positive benefits of greater control over our lives and of embracing the concept of "livelihood" rather than just employment. A human household, through the individuals that compose it, supplies the labor for both paid and unpaid work and also helps create the aggregate demand for economic goods and services. It is the source of "human capital" which tends to be undervalued in the current economic system. Households can have a wide range of monetary status, from luxury to poverty, so it is difficult to generalize or focus on some average or median, but we need to engage to the extent possible across the spectrum—we are all in this together![64]

It has been observed that people in industrial and highly urbanized societies have lost the connection with natural surroundings that their ancestors had. While this is true, we do plant flowers, indoors and outside, and some even raise vegetable gardens. With the trend of population movement toward cities, organizations such as the Nature Conservancy promote environmental enhancements, such as, tree planting for cooling and natural air filtering, continuous greenbelts and stormwater management.[65]

We prize even small yards, along with our parks and open space commons. Although usually far removed from larger wild animals, we still have squirrels, rabbits and a variety of birds even in urban environments. And we cherish our animal pets as part of nature in our homes. Flowers that attract bees and butterflies can be planted, but the main synergistic impact of our household on the ecosystem will come through our collective demand for the necessities of life. An overarching aspect of mindful demand is to reduce waste across the board, and often this can be accomplished through local purchasing which has the incidental benefit of fostering community.

### *Household System Components*

Households can promote synergistic economic effects, some of which may be qualitative, not readily measured, but are nonetheless important to meaningful human lives and preservation of the ecosystem. For example, in human lives a synergistic effect could be joy in using one's capabilities more fully or gratitude for more time spent with loved ones. Ecosystem synergistic effects might be saving a beautiful landscape from development or halting the rapid extinction of species.

### *Food*

Some positive trends in food supply are driven by consumer demand for healthier, sustainable choices and clear product labeling, which highlight the efficiency of the market system in matching supply with demand. Farmers' markets have been around for a good while, but community-supported agriculture (CSA) is a newer choice where subscribers agree to take a portion of a local farmer's production, which varies in type of produce from week to week. There are increasing numbers of community gardens, especially in urban areas where individuals may not have yard space for their own vegetable garden. Natural food groceries, offering both organic and local produce have become increasingly popular, causing supermarkets to offer more and more natural, local and organic choices which in turn has in some cases reduced organic prices to parity with non-organic.

Factory-farmed food generates some health concerns over such things as pesticide residues and growth hormones and it is a major contributor to greenhouse gas emissions (GHG). It is estimated that industrial agriculture accounts for 11-15 percent of GHG, and that food processing, packing and transportation adds another 15-20 percent. On the other hand, regenerative organic farming could sequester a high percentage of annual GHG through adopting widely available and inexpensive practices.[66]

Eating further down the food chain (less beef, more vegetables) is advocated both for health and to reduce GHG.[67] Because of earlier collective consumer action, branded products include dolphin-free tuna; wild-caught seafood; natural meat, eggs and dairy; organic food; whole grains. When producers have resisted clear labeling, consumer action has resulted in such product labels as, gluten-free, non-GMO, and no high fructose corn syrup.

Waste reduction is an area that can have a big positive impact. A recent study shows that in the US 40 percent of our food is wasted! This equates to 1,250 calories per person per day, almost half of our daily recommended requirement, while 42 million Americans have food insecurity and could be fed with just one third of this waste. This waste also equates to 19 percent of our farmland and 21 percent of agricultural water usage. The problem has grown worse over the years, since we now waste about 50 percent more than we did in the 1970s, but there is beginning to be more general awareness of the problem. Food suppliers and restaurants are now becoming engaged with this issue. Forty-three percent of the total waste, or about 17 percent of total food is wasted by households so we can certainly reduce this by being more mindful of not buying more than we can use and doing a better job of using most of what we buy.[68]

We can be proactive in bringing our own fabric shopping bags rather than using the store's plastic or paper, and we can favor green ancilliary products from grocery stores such as cleaning agents and paper products.

### *Shelter*

Shelter is another basic need that could use a serious course correction from the current trend for huge houses that, besides the unwarranted consumption of construction materials, also require excessive energy for heating and cooling. This trend seems to be driven more by status-seeking, measuring self-esteem by the square footage or the cost of one's house, rather than any real need for living space. Proactive consumers could shift this trend toward making less living space, with less time and money required to maintain it, as the more desirable option. This is analogous to the shift away from the high-horsepower, tail-finned autos of the 1950's to the current higher gas mileage, smaller streamline-designed cars.

If we consider the spectrum of housing from apartments to detached single family homes, it can be thought of as trade-offs between amount of living space and the time and money required to maintain it. At one end there is a need for more affordable housing, and at the other there is a good opportunity for sustainability in downsizing. Besides the living space aspect, there can also be greater potential for a synergistic local economy where denser housing fosters robust neighborhood connections and community.

So how might we better address the affordability aspect of housing? To begin, the onset of sharing options is the most efficient approach since it better utilizes existing space. CoAbode matches compatible single mothers with co-housing which permits sharing of childcare, food and other services to lower costs and enable mutual support.[69]

Another approach is sharing senior care facilities by students, with examples both in the U.S. and Europe. There are options for seniors to share space in their home in return for a combination of rent and help with household chores.[70]

There are some initiatives geared to young professionals like the Embassy Network which promotes co-living apartments that combine housing, social connections and career support in the Americas and Europe.[71]

Turning to new construction, it should be noted that besides the trend that emphasizes energy efficiency, there is also attention being given to materials efficiency. The Built Positive movement considers that buildings can serve as material banks, such that components can be disassembled and recovered for other uses when buildings need to be replaced.[72] The authors of *Cradle to Cradle* now operate a certification service that promotes the concept of waste avoidance through product design that results in either biological or technological feedstocks rather than waste. They have developed relationships with both Walmart and Home Depot in this regard.[73]

If we consider more affordable and sustainable home construction, the tiny home movement is being adopted not only by dedicated voluntary simplicity enthusiasts, but also as resources for homeless people. Opportunity Village Eugene, for example, has provided housing for more than 90 people in Eugene, Oregon, since it was founded in 2013. In this case the city donated the land, but there usually needs to be reliance on other land options such as community land trusts for providing affordable housing. These are non-profits that buy urban real estate and keep ownership in trust, while typically leasing parcels for 99 years to low and moderate income people. This permits them to build equity in the housing structures, while protecting them from being displaced in economic downturns or by gentrification. The land trust boards usually have meaningful representation by project residents.[74]

There are now open source building projects like WikiHouse that provide tools for citizens and communities to produce sustainable and affordable homes themselves. With the advent of 3-D printing, also known as additive manufacturing, it is now possible to construct housing both rapidly and more inexpensively saving as much as 30 percent on construction costs.[75]

Three-D printing already has been used to produce a range of structures as large as apartment buildings.[76] A sampling of 3-D printed structures shows a wide variety, and there are expectations that future developments can utilize scrap plastics and recycled concrete.[77]

The most prominent model for housing construction that involves sweat equity is Habitat for Humanity. It offers financially accessible options of various types in exchange for hands-on work for the project. It also accepts donations of used furniture, appliances and building materials thereby eliminating some landfill wastes.[78] Perhaps this model could be expanded to provide summer jobs for students in high school and college as a means of building up "credits" for future housing access.

Looking at the problem of wasteful, excessively large houses, we already see countervailing trends. Proactive, consumer demand for smaller houses is on the rise. Large, far-flung houses that required long commutes became liabilities during the 2008 oil price spike; some have even been demolished.[79] In some cases, oversize suburban houses are amenable to being reconfigured as multi-family dwellings as has happened to large urban townhouses. Online shopping is having the same effect on large retail malls. Some malls are being repurposed to other uses as, earlier, had been the case with abandoned industrial lofts.[80]

Finally, it has been shown that people have a natural affinity for smaller, more personal living spaces and in some cases this has produced ordinances against McMansions. With smaller dwellings and less storage space there may be a beneficial side-effect for less accumulation of "stuff." At the end of the day, a proactive choice for a smaller house would pay dividends in fewer materials used in construction, lower energy usage and less personal time required to maintain it.

### *Utilities*

Energy and water are the main utilities used to operate our households and are, therefore, a prime focus for reducing waste and taking important steps toward sustainability and a Life-Centered Economy.

Looking first at energy, we know that between 30 to 50 percent of the electricity produced by large scale, centralized generation reaches consumers. Natural gas is a more efficiently transported source of energy for home heating and cooking. About 90 percent of its energy potential reaches the consumer.[81]

Eight to 15 percent of centralized electricity production is lost in transmission, which points up the advantage of locally installed solar panels.[82] In a positive trend some utilities are beginning to give their customers some choice for sourcing electricity from renewables. For example, XCEL in Colorado has offered a 100 percent wind option at about a 12 percent cost premium, with lower premiums for lesser percentages, as well as some solar options. But even renewable sources like wind and solar, that do not use fossil fuels, would be more efficient if located closer to the point of consumption so as to minimize transmission losses.

Looking at existing housing space, there are sustainability improvements that can be made to even older dwellings. These can be simply upgrading replacement items like light bulbs and appliances and "do-it-yourself" caulking around windows and doors.[83] There are also more sophisticated options that can be considered as time and money permit, such as solar panels on the roof and upgrades of insulation, lighting, and appliances. The upgrades can be done as replacements over time to minimize upfront costs. Tools such as smart thermostats and apps for appliances that are controllable by smart phones can make a big impact on energy efficiency.[84]

Utility companies are using behavioural motivation to reduce energy use. By compiling information on household energy consumption within neighborhoods, they are encouraging compliance with "social norms. This has proven to reduce energy use and, therefore, the need to build additional power plants. This approach with 95 utilities in nine counties saved enough energy to take the state of New Hampshire off the grid for a year.[85] This type of motivation might be applied to lowering carbon footprints.

Renewables provide a combined benefit of sustainable energy, job creation, and a potential focal point for a community-based economy through a local solar micro-grid cooperative—synergism in action!

A DOE report showed that in 2016 solar was creating more US electricity jobs than oil, gas, coal, and nuclear combined.[86] The cost of electricity from photovoltaic panels fell by 75 percent and from onshore wind by 30 percent from 2009- 2017.[87]

With new technologies supporting rooftop solar, like blockchain accounting and home batteries, new user-driven decentralized energy systems are emerging that can work in tandem with the traditional large-scale electrical grid such as the Brooklyn Micro-Grid project.[88] Some intermediaries like Guzman Energy help small municipal utilities and rural energy cooperatives both save costs and access clean energy sources.[89]

By 2017, 25 states had at least one community solar project in the works, and some of these were utilizing former landfills, such as, the two-megawatt Pikes Peak Solar Garden in Colorado.[90]

In Minnesota there is a program that allows utility customers to purchase shares of local solar facilities, which has generated a large number of solar co-ops.[91]

Namaste Solar is a worker co-op that has evolved into a multi-state operation as it shares the economic benefits of the renewable energy transition with workers.[92]

There is a water/energy nexus—it takes energy to supply water and it takes water for certain types of energy generation. Saving water also saves energy![93] The Pacific Institute even provides a calculator to help save both.[94]

Utilities are also using the behavioral motivation methods which is helping to reduce water consumption, especially for outdoor applications which can be half of all household usage.[95]

Some cities in semi-arid regions take drastic action like Las Vegas, which pays households to remove grass lawns and use xeriscape instead with drought-resistant plants and rocks. By 2014, after 12 years of the program, water use had been cut by one-third while the population increased by one-fifth. All water used indoors is also recycled.[96]

Besides featuring many water-saving products that potentially could cut household water consumption by 50 percent, *Consumer Reports* shows a graph of water consumption by use with lawns at 29 percent nationally, followed by toilets at 19 percent, washers at 15 percent, showers at 12 percent, faucets at 11 percent and leaks at 10 percent.[97]

Many of the paths to more sustainable consumption of both energy and water can be undertaken with very little time and effort, and mainly require a more mindful approach to how we conduct our daily lives. It would seem that the likely development of local solar energy micro-grid cooperatives would have the added benefit of developing a more cohesive sense of community in our increasingly urbanized society, much as the successful 1936 Rural Electrification Act, which provided federal loans for cooperative electric power companies.[98]

### *Lifestyle Goods*

This area encompasses such things as clothing, furnishings and equipment. Big ticket items that relate to lifestyle such as houses and cars are discussed elsewhere. But it is in this sector that proactive consumers can perhaps have the largest impact for personal empowerment and satisfaction as well as for the greater good.

We are a long way from the Depression-era slogan of "use it up, wear it out, make do or do without" when frugality was deemed a virtue. However, we can still be mindful of the effect of our purchases on the health of the planet and the good of society. We have at our disposal an ever-increasing amount of product information via brands, "green" certifications, recyclability, etc. that can inform our choices. Moreover, we have organizations such as Green America and Consumers Report that not only provide product information, but also focus concerted consumer power to promote safe and sustainable products.

It is in this sector of the economy that advertising is especially geared to support planned obsolescence – to create demand for the next new fashion or the gadget with more features. But this is also the sector where we can exert our individuality, and "just say no" to the latest thing that is pushed at us. Will it really deliver the satisfaction it promises over the item we already possess? If we have to add to an unpaid credit card balance to obtain it, do we really want to spend more of our time working to pay outrageous interest charges that enrich big banks? Those in more affluent circumstances can be trendsetters for a more mindful and simpler lifestyle, living within planetary limits both now and for future generations.

### Clothing

In her book, *The Story of Stuff,* Annie Leonard chronicles the environmental and societal impacts of producing a simple cotton T-shirt and getting it to market. She details the water consumed, the chemicals applied, the developing country labor exploited, the transportation involved and the carbon dioxide generated. While noting that organic and fair trade products are a better choice, the "best" choice is to wear out the T-shirt you have before buying a new one.[99]

Annie Leonard says that she is often asked: what should one buy? Of course it is best to buy "green" products if possible, but she also advocates for active citizenship to promote systemic changes for sustainability, saying that while green consumerism is certainly important, much more than that is needed if we are to live within our ecological limits.[100]

The siren call to buy the latest fashion, and plump up some pseudo self-esteem, can be resisted. Instead an example can be set for our children and friends to do likewise and resist these impulses. When we do need to purchase clothing, we can be guided by information for sustainable and ethical choices.[101]

### Furnishings

In the book, *Cradle to Cradle,* the authors advocate for products designed that, when they come to end of their useful life, they can be recycled into feedstocks for new products instead of becoming waste.[102] This concept is taking root, with

Shaw Industries, the world's largest carpet company, now having 85 percent of their products cradle-to-cradle certified, and recent support from both Walmart and Home Depot as previously mentioned.[103]

With furniture in particular, it may be advantageous to consider second-hand products as well as the above certifications. Older furniture was often manufactured to last, even for generations, and the craftsmanship is hard to duplicate in modern manufacturing. It can be refinished and reupholstered along the way, and that supports local repair shops. The well-advertised latest styling can be resisted in favor of a more durable range of products that add to a dwelling's ambience over time.

We might be especially mindful of minimizing the use of plastics, except where they are clearly recyclable. They account for about four percent of petroleum products consumed worldwide as feedstocks, and another four percent for powering manufacturing processes, for a total of eight percent. Only a small portion is currently made from plant sources.[104] We should also avoid species of woods from tropical endangered rainforests, which can include some species of teak, ebony and rosewood.[105]

### *Equipment*

This sector includes a range of manufactured products, from appliances to cell phones. *Consumer Reports* does a good job of evaluating many of these items in terms of utility, safety, and environmental impact.

For the larger appliances, ratings can be found for parameters such as energy and water consumption, along with functional aspects. Most items in this category are bought as replacements for broken or worn out equipment. However entertainment items, such as TVs and stereo systems, are subject to advertising-pushed upgrades that often do not deliver a commensurate increase in satisfaction.

Considering personal equipment like cell phones and computers, there has been a concerted industry promotion of upgrades. But with today's faster and more capable gadgets, it is possible to keep them much longer with only a very modest amount of maintenance and periodic component replacement.[106]

Efforts are being made to identify gold and tantalum used in some electronic devices that are mined under conditions of violent conflict and terrible worker exploitation, particularly in the Democratic Republic of the Congo in Africa. However, it is often difficult for manufacturers to determine the source of the metals they are using. This is another good reason to recycle electronic devices and help minimize the extraction of these non-renewable metals.[107]

### *Sustainable Suppliers*

Thankfully, there are a growing number of enterprises dedicated to serving all their stakeholders in a sustainable way. A notable example is the large, farmer-owned Organic Valley cooperative that provides eggs and dairy products while preserving family farms.[108] B Corporations are another positive development. B Corporations are a new kind of business; they are legally required to consider the impact of their decisions on their workers, customers, suppliers, communities and the environment.

This is a worldwide voluntary movement of business leaders to use their enterprises as force for good. As of August 2018, there were over 2,600 certified B Corporations across 150 industries in 60 countries.[109] A sampling of well-known, certified B Corporations include, Patagonia, Seventh Generation, Ben & Jerry's, New Belgium Brewing, Etsy and Dansko. Energy Star and Organic certifications also indicate goods that have been produced taking stakeholder value into account rather than just shareholder value.[110]

Attention and patronage should also be directed to local craft, small-scale manufacturers and repair shops that may be organized as cooperatives, locally owned corporations, and proprietorships. Not only is customer service generally better in smaller enterprises than in big box stores, but the money spent tends to circulate in support of the local economy rather than being siphoned off to a distant headquarters.

### *Transportation*

In transportation, individual choices are greatly influenced by the built infrastructure where one lives. In daily lives, the options may include cars, buses, trains, bicycles and walking. Possible distant travel options are cars, buses, trains and airplanes. However, regardless of the particular location, there are still choices that can minimize the non-human energy used and the environmental impact. Often these choices involve trade-offs between time and money, and some locations may provide only limited options.

The ubiquitous automobile makes the biggest impact on energy and the environment. A good starting point for reducing impact is to minimize usage with some common sense actions. Errands can be combined with a little planning, and that saves time as well as reducing energy consumption and pollution. Ride sharing by commuters can save both time and money by using dedicated toll lanes with reduced or free toll costs and faster traffic flow, besides reducing personal shares of automobile operating and maintenance costs.

Besides ride sharing, there is a growing trend of car sharing via mobility services like Lyft and Uber, where a driver is involved, and Car2Go where the customer picks up and drops off a vehicle via a more flexible car rental service for metro areas. There have been concerns about both driver exploitation and harm to passengers from unvetted drivers from services such as Lyft and Uber, and some cities have begun to regulate them more closely. In Austin, Texas, this resulted in both companies pulling out of that market whereupon new alternatives such as Ride Austin began offering services that addressed those concerns. In San Francisco, city ordinances were modified in 2010 to require new developments to provide parking spaces for car-sharing providers. This has proved successful as shown in a 2017 evaluation for local firms such as Zipcar and Getaround.. These are round-trip services and there is sentiment to extend this concept to one-way services like Car2Go.[111]

Purchasing an automobile is a large expenditure second only to purchasing a house. Depending on one's financial resources, small cars with good gas mileage, hybrid gas/electric battery cars and all-electric battery cars each provide some benefits related to fossil-fuel energy and the environment. With battery prices having already fallen by more than half since 2011 and projected to continue a steep decline, there does seem to be the beginning of a strong trend favoring electric vehicles.

What needs to happen for electric cars to take over transportation? There are some obstacles that will need to be overcome: providing sufficient mineral resources for battery production, lowering the initial cost of electric cars, a major restructuring of auto manufacturing and repair services, and developing a comprehensive infrastructure of charging stations. The ecological benefits from electric vehicles will be highly dependent on the energy source for the electricity, that is, renewables—not fossil fuels.[112]

Can we be moving beyond the car culture? There are some signs of a beginning transition. Many younger Americans are not planning to own a car, deeming it an unnecessary expense. As public transit options increase, there are more reasons to question the need for a car that sits in the garage most of the time—or scale back to just one car. It seems that automakers are now devoting attention to "the first mile/last mile" category and this includes the new emphasis on driverless cars for ride-hailing services. GM has already partnered with Lyft, and the focus on mobility services has even moved to bicycles with Ford aiming for 7000 branded bikes in San Francisco during 2018.[113]

Some cities are supporting the move toward transportation alternatives from reliance on cars alone. Minneapolis has a Guaranteed Ride Home Program that is available to anyone commuting to work or school at least three times per week by train, bus, car- or van-pool, bicycle, or walking. It takes the form of a city-sponsored "commuter insurance" for $100 a year for four rides home in case an unexpected event makes the normal commute impossible.[114] Denver and Boulder, Colorado, have given grants to a non-profit, CarShare, to create a Multi-modal Toolkit. It combines discounted public transit passes, car-sharing programs, and bike-sharing memberships along with information on how best to utilize them. The program ran from spring 2014 to February 2016 and 75 percent of the toolkit recipients made use of it.[115] Portland, Oregon, launched a 1000-bike and 100-station sharing program in July of 2016 and made plans to roll out an adaptive bike option for the physically disabled in 2017. The city has also sponsored educational events to expand participation in this initiative.[116]

Walking can be encouraged where feasible through manageable distances and sidewalks or footpaths. An innovative "walking school bus" program began in Australia but has spread to Europe and the US. It is organized as a free service, with a ratio of one adult to eight students ideal, and any student can participate whether or not their parent has volunteered as one of the "drivers." This can be as simple or elaborate as the participants choose, but has the benefits of safe passage, exercise and social interaction besides saving non-human energy and eliminating pollution.[117] A 2011 study showed that randomly chosen students in the Houston, Texas, area increased their participation by 38 percent over a five-week period.[118]

When transportation for long trips is considered, the energy consumption analysis needs to be on a comparable basis. A recent report by the International Council on Clean Transportation focuses on a 300-500 mile trip where the choice of transport might be car, plane, bus or rail. This shows planes as least efficient, at 43 passenger miles per gallon gasoline equivalent (MPGge), followed by Amtrak trains at 51, cars at 52 and Greyhound buses the very best at 152 MPGge.[119]

### *Communications*

We are fortunate to have an unprecedented host of communication tools at our disposal, many of them Internet-related. These include regular cell phones, smart phones, tablets, laptops, desktop computers and multi-channel TV hardware as well as all manner of applications (apps) like email, social media, video-conferencing and search engines. As a result we have very broad access to information and interpersonal connections. Like many tools, they can bring positive benefits but can also have some negative impacts.

Some Silicon Valley technical experts have begun pushing back at the addictive behavior that some apps can foster.[120] There is also concern that apps like Facebook can cause alienation through constant social comparison rather than building positive relationships.[121]

The growing problem of disinformation or "fake news" shows a pressing need to educate the public to discern true information. The Associated Press is now working with Facebook to combat misinformation.[122] Already some states are addressing this need through an initial focus on school curricula.[123]

There is a greatly enhanced access to knowledge that years ago would have been almost impossible to duplicate via the library system. Search engines like Google can bring up an online encyclopedia, Wikipedia, and many other reference sources for the search topic.[124] Beyond such searches, there are increasing opportunities for Massive Online Open Courses (MOOC) that cover a wide range of subjects and are either free or available at modest costs. This movement is supplementing existing college offerings, and paving the way for more specifically focused education, whether for needed occupational skills or continuing adult education.[125]

Another emerging application is the digital delivery of healthcare through smartphone apps. Besides saving trips to doctor's offices, some apps can gather and send patient data as well as delivering medical services. An example would be MySugar which helps diabetics manage their condition. In 2016 the US Food & Drug Administration approved 36 connected health apps and devices. Kaiser Permanente says that in 2016 more than half of its doctor-patient interactions were via video conference or text messages.[126]

Perhaps one of the best aspects of our communication options, in terms of reducing energy consumption and environmental impact, are the video conferencing options such as Skype and Zoom. These can offer an attractive alternative to long distance travel, whether for business or visiting family and friends. They are either free or low cost, and can provide the extra aspects of communication from visual contact that sound alone does not offer. Besides serving as an alternative to long distance trips, videoconferencing has become a very useful tool for telecommuting and for participating in the gig economy.

However, much of the advance in communication options depends on a continued viable Internet. It was developed initially with public money and evolved in an open source fashion, but has become increasingly privatized in the US. Not only has this led to higher prices, but poor and rural communities are underserved. Thirty-nine percent of rural Americans lack broadband, and nearly half of households with less than $30,000 per year income lack any access, especially among black and Hispanic households. Fortunately, there is an alternative—municipal broadband. Chattanooga is the best example, but there are other cities across the country with similar initiatives.[127]

There is a growing movement by Rural Electric Cooperatives to provide broadband in rural areas, much as they did for electricity.[128]

In any case, continued strong grassroots support will be needed in order to keep the Internet as a viable tool for citizen and consumer activism. If current efforts by big Internet service providers to eliminate net neutrality succeed, it would require higher prices for higher speed access and thus limit the usefulness for many public interest groups. From flash protests against an immigration ban to the Women's March, Internet-based communication was a key tool for their organization. Online petitions on behalf of both engaged citizens and proactive consumers could be stifled through pro-business regulation by government or by the businesses themselves.[129]

## *Labor Supply*

The household continues to be the main source of labor supply, but the nature of the work that is performed continues to evolve. In the book *Future Work,* James Robertson depicts an historical progression from slavery to serfdom to employment, and now a transition from employment to what he terms "own work." The employment model will certainly continue to provide many jobs, but we can expect a trend of combining conventional employment with own work. He sees this as a liberating development with increasing numbers of people deciding to do "their own thing" and finding ways to do it.[130]

The focus above is on labor that is expended externally from the household. There is also a great deal of labor that is expended within the household for cooking, cleaning, childcare, eldercare, and maintenance. This usually falls in the category of unpaid work. With the trend toward consumer-driven materialism that began after World War II, there are more and more households with multiple members engaged in external work. This has had some good impacts in opening more career opportunities for women, who bore the brunt of the unpaid internal work, and in driving more synergy within the household such that men share in more of the internal work. However, the materialistic drive for more "stuff" has also led to unsustainable economic growth.

## *Transition Considerations*

More recently there have been some trends that will be disruptive to the current employment model and are already having an impact. With off-shoring of jobs via globalization and the increasing utilization of robotics, conventional employment is shrinking. With the Internet as a tool there are more options for telecommuting, but also more of a need to be "on call" more constantly. We are both working longer and being more inequitably compensated.

A 2014 survey showed that Americans worked 47 hours per week on average, and one fifth work as much as 59 hours per week. Interestingly, it showed that workers in the higher skilled occupations like law and business management worked the longest hours. But these categories also exhibited the most inequality between high- and low-paid workers. The fear of being replaced is a driver for the long hours. Often in lower-skilled occupations, workers are not permitted to work long hours, so they can be kept on part-time status without benefits.[131]

The survey did not show this, but it is likely that many of these workers take on a second or even third job to make ends meet, and therefore also work long hours.

The current employment model also skews the rewards for time worked in an increasingly unequal fashion, as shown in the following examples. "In 2015, the median CEO pay package for 200 large US companies was almost $20 million per year, nearly 400 times the pay of a typical worker."[132] If we assume a 2000 hour work-year, this equates to $10,000 per hour or $80,000 for one day's work—an income that would satisfy many for one year! This compares to only a 20:1 ratio in 1965. Most of the benefits of increased productivity have been passed on to shareholders rather than workers—real wages have been flat for decades.

The rise of the Internet-based gig economy offers flexibility and a new range of opportunities, but so far the enabling online platforms have been dominated by large corporations such as Amazon and Uber that offer little or no worker benefits such as health insurance, pensions, and employment security.

However, a combination of the emerging platform cooperative movement, local economic development initiatives, startup collectives, and responsible sharing-based organizations is offering a viable path forward, which is supportive of a life-centered economy.[133] The growing momentum for "platform cooperativism" provides an alternative for users, rather than corporations, to control online platforms such as websites and apps. Some examples of successful platform co-ops include Modo, a Canadian car-sharing co-op; Stocksy United, an online artist-owned co-op; and Green Taxi Cooperative in Denver, Colorado.[134]

New York City launched the Worker Cooperative Business Development Initiative in 2015, that then doubled the number of worker co-ops in its first year, and led to an increase in funding for 2016 from $1.2 to $2.1 million. Evergreen in Cleveland, Ohio, is a longer established network of worker co-ops, linked together by a non-profit holding corporation. These include a green industrial laundry, a solar installation and energy efficiency retrofitting company and a large commercial greenhouse.[135]

Another trend is found in local production that creates some synergy between consumers and producers, and develops "prosumers." This maker culture is served by such organizations as Fab Lab, developed at MIT in the US.[136] The concept is to provide the latest tools and machines for collaborative production to support a distributed international network of scientific researchers and community inventors. What gets designed to benefit one local community can theoretically be fabricated in another lab anywhere in the world. Having begun in India as the first location outside of MIT, it has spread to 665 Fab Labs in 65 countries.[137]

### Re-imagining Household Labor: A Time Perspective

In his essay on *The Joyful Economy*, Gus Speth focuses on local life. He expects that the new joyful economy will be rooted in the community and region, with production of a range of items, but especially food and energy supplies. It will be supported by local complementary currency and local financial institutions. People will be closer to work outside the household, allowing for more walking and biking. This scenario will allow households to participate more fully in local governance of institutions and our commons. He envisions that formal work hours will be reduced and thus free up time for household production, continuing education, interaction with family and friends, volunteering and recreation. "Life will be less frenetic. Frugality and thrift will be prized and wastefulness shunned. Mindfulness and living simply with less clutter will carry the day."[138]

Time banks and similar care banks (focused on child and elder care) have arisen as tools to facilitate community-centered services, but are not a total solution. Time bank principles are as follows:

Assets – We are all assets.

Redefining Work – Some work is beyond price.

Reciprocity – Helping works better as a two-way street.

Social Networks – We need each other.

Respect – Every human being matters.

For time banks, all time is valued equally so an hour of plumbing would be the same as an hour of lawn-mowing. Care banks are similar, but as in a Japanese system, different values can apply to some tasks. For example, household chores have a lower value than attending to the personal care of others. Some people even donate time as a charitable contribution and do not make withdrawals.[139]

In *The Locust and the Bee* Geoff Mulgan notes that despite the current money-centered system discounting the future, we do not run our lives that way in many respects. We invest in our children, support education, and donate to capital projects for organizations that we support with no expectation of a financial return. He notes that some countries use a very low or zero discount rate for healthcare decisions, feeling that younger generations should not be disadvantaged in comparison to older ones by imputing higher future costs.[140]

It is interesting to realize that if we participate in community on a volunteer or "gift" basis, we do not discount the future in the way the current system does. If I shovel snow for my neighbor, he will likely return the favor in the future, but if the transaction is monetized, and one party is paid, studies show that discharges the obligation.[141]

Mulgan's article "Time Rather Than Money," considers some interrelationships between time and money that speak to a Life-Centered rather than a Money-Centered Economy:

> *"If time becomes the primary, and most visible currency of life, what follows? Money is frozen time: capital is frozen work."*

Mulgan compares some aspects of the current system with a time-oriented system and speculates on the implications of the latter. It may encompass both meaningful human life cycles and longer cycles of ecological time. He notes that numbers in the current system are time-based—discounted, forecast, and hedged—and asks how such mechanisms could be used in service of the quality of lived time.

*"There are some simple implications, many of which are already visible.*

*"If as much attention is paid to time as is now paid to money, we can expect proliferations of time accounts, time banks, time exchanges, time rights and time credits. All of these instruments allow people to store time or to swap it with others.*

*"We might expect ever more rights linked to time – including rights to paid and unpaid leave, rights to training time, rights to adjust the fixed hours of the working week.*

*"We might expect educational institutions devoted to helping people use time more effectively. Imagine schools of life as well as schools to prepare for work and coaches skilled in pointing out to people how they might use their time more effectively.*

*"None of these are fantasies or utopian. All exist already, though on nothing like the scale of their equivalents in and around money.*

*"Finally, a society that was more attentive to time would reverse the relationship between time and money that is found in contemporary economics. Time is the servant of money, there to be carved up, measured and managed in order to increase monetary profit.*

*"So what would happen if the relationship was inverted, and money became the servant of our aspiration for more and better time? That's the brave new world to aspire to."*[142]

### Money

The main functions of money have been described as follows:

1) Medium of exchange (replacing barter)
2) Unit of account (pricing mechanism)
3) Storage of value
4) Earning capacity (under present system money earns interest)

A fifth indirect function has also developed over time, and that is a measure of status or self-esteem.

Money facilitates synergism within the economic system as it connects buyers, sellers, investors and businesses. However, money should be the servant of a Life-Centered Economy, not the master which it apparently is becoming. A good perspective on money in terms of life energy is provided in the book, *Your Money or Your Life*.[143]

If we consider our household activities, we engage with money in many ways. Very basically there are income and expenditures, with income being derived from wages and investments and expenditures categorized as mandatory and discretionary. There are also a number of institutions and tools with which we interact in dealing with money.

If we live in an area with a local currency, use of it provides good synergy in support of the local businesses that accept it.[144] These local currencies serve as an alternative to the national currency and operate in parallel (not as a replacement). A familiar example of an alternative currency is frequent traveler points. These can be used not only for air travel, but for hotels, rental cars, and a wide range of purchases.

We need to store our money somewhere, and this choice can be a local or regional bank or credit union rather than a big Wall Street bank so that the money nourishes local enterprise. There is a movement to expand the public banking option, pioneered by North Dakota, and this option even more directly benefits the local economy by channeling local or state government funds into their respective infrastructure needs.[145] There has also been a trend to move from traditional banks to credit unions, which generally offer lower fees and better savings rates than banks, and now have over 100 million members.[146] Some focus specifically on serving the local community, as does the Self-Help Credit Union, founded in Durham, NC. It has expanded by merging with similar organizations across the country into a larger network called the Self-Help Federal Credit Union.[147]

### *Debt*

The credit card is perhaps the single tool that is most responsible for driving excessive consumption and consumer debt. It offers the instant gratification of making a purchase even if you do not have the money in hand to do so. Therefore, instead of saving up for a purchase as earlier generations did before the widespread use of credit cards, we can enjoy the item now and pay later—so easy! Unfortunately, some people are unable to pay their credit card balances in full and then are hit with high interest charges, which can be over 20 percent. They accumulate more and more debt over time. This impact is not as severe as that of payday lenders keeping people in perpetual debt, but it affects a great many more people.

There is an effort by credit card companies to eliminate cash and check purchase options so as to force even greater use of credit cards. In addition to the profound debt implications, credit card use can track personal information, most often without user awareness, and also expose them to fraud as in the Wells Fargo case.[148]

As we age and move through our lives, we also encounter some larger structured debt obligations. The rise of student loans to pay for excessive, out of control education costs has saddled many young people with the equivalent of a small mortgage (which includes a ban on debt discharge through bankruptcy) as they graduate from colleges. There is popular support to rein in this burden on graduates. A recent study shows that a federally financed debt cancellation program would have a meaningful positive impact on the national economy.[149]

The other major discretionary debt situations involve housing and transportation. In order to afford a house to raise a family, mortgage financing is almost a necessity for most people. However, the cost of a house can be greatly influenced by the buyer's requirements. We can be secure in our self-esteem, rather than measuring it by the size of the house and yard, and focus instead on those aspects that we truly need. Likewise, if we need to buy a car, it can be equipped to meet our needs rather than to stroke our ego. Moreover, we can benefit greatly by keeping the car for many years rather than trading it every two years and absorbing the heaviest depreciation loss in value.

### *Investments*

Socially responsible investing has matured over the last three decades from a simple exclusion of "sin stocks" such as tobacco, liquor, and gun producers to incorporate a wide range of environmental, social and corporate governance issues, or E.S.G. From being driven initially by consumer activists, this concept has entered the mainstream and captured the attention of large investors who are concerned about the impact of E.S.G. on future earnings. MSCI, a leading provider of market indices, takes a sophisticated approach and does not eliminate all stocks in a given category for its rankings. For example, among oil companies MSCI ranks Norwegian Statoil highly due to its good environmental practices, but ranks American Chevron low due to its high environmental risk profile. It is worth noting that investment performance does not necessarily suffer with choices that promote economic synergism with people and planet.[150]

Another example of investor activism is the vote at Exxon's annual shareholder meeting in 2017 to require annual reporting on the business impact of global measures taken to keep climate change below a two-degree-Centigrade temperature increase. It passed by a two-to-one margin.[151] There are even calls for mutual fund managers to take into account the negative correlation between overpaid CEOs and company performance, in an effort to rein in excessive compensation.[152]

Another encouraging mainstream trend is the divestment from fossil fuel producers. In late 2017 the Norwegian sovereign fund said it was considering such a move despite the fact that most of its revenue had come from North Sea oil. Then the European insurance giant Axa said it would divest $825 million in Canadian tar sand oil production and pipelines. Most importantly, the World Bank said that by 2019 it would no longer fund oil and gas exploration. There is also a trend for cities to divest from banks like Wells Fargo that underwrite pipeline projects like the Dakota Access pipeline, and environmental groups continue to pressure banks to stop financing the Keystone XL pipeline.[153]

So the influence of a lot of consumer activism is bearing fruit, and households have more opportunities to direct their investments in support of a synergistic Life-Centered Economy. *Green American* has a wealth of resources for socially responsible investing by households. They also point out that we can influence the investment direction of organizations we belong to such as our workplaces and faith congregations.[154]

We need to bear in mind that money is a means to an end, not the end itself, and we can replace "love of money" with "love of life".

## *Conclusion*

This chapter has discussed the many ways that human households and their communities can embrace economic synergism, an approach that promotes wellbeing for its participants and the ecosystem in which they reside. The basic elements of food, shelter, utilities, lifestyle goods, transportation, communication, labor supply, and money are all addressed from this new perspective. The means are in hand to pursue all these changes. We have the tools we require and do not need anyone's permission. We will not all pursue every one of these initiatives, but for the ones we choose, we can empower ourselves and overcome manipulation by the current system.

Speth's vision in *A Joyful Economy*, is that a range of hybrid business models will develop along with the rise of more business incubators. The profit motive can be supplanted with more emphasis on social and public good, along with environmental responsibility. Consumerism can become replaced by the search for things that truly bring happiness and fulfillment—family and friends, enjoyment of nature and meaningful work that engages our individual potentials. Overconsumption can be shunned and more energy can be directed to community and the commons. [155]

If enough of us pursue this path to a synergistic Life-Centered Economy, then "growth in GDP will be taken off its pedestal and replaced by children"—our future generations. Instead of GDP, new indicators of true wellbeing will be used both for the present and the long term. Although we will have returned to a more localized and regionalized economy, a heightened awareness and engagement with global issues will also be possible—and very necessary!

# CHAPTER 4
# How Do We Get There? Transition to the Life-Centered Economy

## Background and Assumptions

To transition to a life-centered, synergistic economy, it is not necessary to create a whole new economic theory or system, but rather to build on the strengths and assets of our current system. Large radical changes are not necessary, but small actions that taken together generate powerful shifts in the economic structure and the relationships that underlie that structure.

A few assumptions support our economic framework for change. The first is that we embrace the power of "true capitalism". At its best capitalism has shown that it is a highly effective mechanism for the efficient use of resources, recognizes the power and reality of self-interest, and is decentralized. For capitalism to operate at its best, however, several attributes are required, all of which were embedded in Adam Smith's primary analysis.[156] First, capitalism relies on competition between small-scale entrepreneurs, none of whom have a dominant share of the market. Capital must be distributed among the various economic players so that it is not centralized too much in any one place or person. The entrepreneurs themselves must have some underlying value structure that includes basic ethics of how business is done and recognizes the common good ("public virtue" in the words of Adam Smith). It also relies on the availability of information on pricing and product quality.

Two current major trends build on the effectiveness of capitalism. The first is the trend toward local markets in consumption, production, and finance. Both public desire and public infrastructure are improving to support these. The information available with the rise of the Internet allows for easy comparison of product information and prices. This facilitates decentralized economic activity. Jeremy Rifkin has gone so far as to note the potential for a production capacity with essentially zero marginal cost of key goods and services.[157]

"Prosumers" create a "collaborative commons" interconnected with the capitalist market system. While taken to the extremes this seems unrealistic, it is important to realize that the Internet, 3-D printers, and other new systems and technologies allow us to think differently and distribute goods and services more effectively and democratically.

Binary economics or "cooperative economics" recognizes the existence of both human (labor) and nonhuman (capital) forces within the economic system and thus the critical importance of sharing and decentralization of capital itself. Participatory, distributive, and social justice is key to restoring our own sense of agency within our lives and within the economy.

Expectations play a considerable role in the health of the economy and our own personal health. It is import to promote and inspire hope and to believe in possibilities for self and societal improvement. The ability to make a difference by our own actions and participation in society is fundamental to a thriving community and economy. We must pay attention to the nature of relationships and structures that promote positive expectations.

The power inherent in all of these is that they are self-organizing, primarily decentralized, and build, rather than tear down, relationships and community. They do not rely on any major government intervention nor on the support of large monopolistic corporate entities. They focus on the economic and relational synergism that is inherent in nature herself.

However, there is no "one size fits all" approach to the economic and relationship transition being proposed. What works in one geographic area or culture may not work exactly the same or at all in another. The concept of "Ba" or the shared space that creates a foundation for knowledge creation and interaction is different within space and time.[158] While this may seem a bit esoteric, it is important to seek the underlying context that guides our work and existence, and to immerse ourselves in the current reality, its structures, relationships, and history.

Therefore, we must pay attention to our way of thinking as well. Systems theory and ideas around community ecology must be integrated into the overarching model. While decentralized and small-scale activities tend to minimize impact and promote positive relational effects, it is important to be aware of the nature of interconnectedness and feedback loops more so than the simple belief in "root causes".

## *Emerging Processes and Mechanisms*

Building on these core economic paradigms, we can focus our personal and collective energies on many effective examples that are already happening. These processes promote community and positive relationships and processes that support the underlying economic mechanisms and theories noted above.

### *Community*

Current theory about community notes the ideal size required to maintain good social relationships to be around 150. It is important then that we consider economic mechanisms that allow for connections in various smaller groupings. Healthy vibrant communities require engaged participation, meaningful work, and true economic and social agency.

What then are some emerging or established means to encourage this kind of healthy connectivity? How is a sense of true community maintained rather than disconnected? What allows for a sense of mutual connection/affection between human beings so there is a shared sense of common vision and reciprocity?

First, processes area needed that support community dialogue and deliberation. In the last twenty years a strong healthy networks have developed that promote the engagement of individuals with one another in decisions about their future. Networks, such as, the National Coalition for Dialogue and Deliberation,[159] the University Network for Collaborative Governance, the Deliberative Democracy Coalition, the National Civic League, the Participatory Budget Project,[160] the Parliament of World Religions and others are developing the tools and capacity for a wide range of ways for individuals and groups to engage civilly with one another in participatory democracy.

### *Empowering and Engaging Participation*

The National Coalition for Dialogue and Deliberation[159] is a network of individuals and organization that create processes and tools to create more unity in tackling societies tough issues.

Participatory Budgeting[160] builds into government decision making systematic processes for community members to actively set financial priorities.

These tools for deliberation and dialogue allow members of the community to directly engage in developing visions and public policy for their community. Statewide projects such as Envision Utah, TBD Colorado and Oregon's Kitchen Cabinet and Oregon Consensus have been championed by their state governors. Other cities and neighborhoods have created processes in which citizens have final, direct say in how their taxes dollars are spent, voting for their priorities. These processes allow for individuals to connect at different levels, find consensus, and build community.

Healthy and successful community organizing led by groups, such as, the Industrial Areas Foundation and the

PICO National Network, are building neighborhood and community capacity to enact change. In the past, many of these organizing projects have been highly adversarial. However, now they are empowering communities to take a stand while also leveraging the various assets and networks within the neighborhoods and regions where they work.

Social media like Nextdoor.com and others allow neighbors to connect on everything from lost animals to the placement of new businesses and economic development.

Communities are incorporating concepts of restorative justice into their local justice systems, allowing for just treatment of both victim and perpetrator and the healing of the community relationships that have been broken as a result of a crime. Retributive justice tends to split communities by marginalizing certain groups and disengages families and others from each other. Instead, schools and local judges are supporting Restorative Justice programs that decrease legal and prison costs, as well as creating networks that support both the victim and offender.

## Economic Units and Processes

Economic processes are best when they maintain a small scale or allow for the independent interaction of systems like blockchain mechanisms that provide checks and balances on large governments and corporations. *Small is Beautiful* by E.F. Schumacher[161] is as relevant today as it was in 1973. We must build economics systems "as if people mattered".

What are these vibrant economic systems at work today? First there are those that build on the best of capitalism, developing truly competitive local markets and financial investment that are focused locally and/or sustainably.

Foundations that support local investment are taking the lead in keeping money within local economies through their support of investment pools, social innovation funds, the promotion of anchor institutions and community wealth building.

## *Local Investment*

Calvert Impact Capital, for example, has initiated Ours to Own initiatives in three different cities (Minneapolis/St. Paul, Denver, and Baltimore). For as little as $20 individuals can invest in a way that ensures their money is going to support local businesses and services.[162] Foundations and private companies are supporting communities through social innovation funds. Rose Community Foundation's Colorado Nonprofit Social Enterprise Exchange[163] and the Denver Foundations Social Venture Capital Partners have shown how training and start up investment can have a major impact on local groups working to generate income.[164] The number and diversity of social investment funds have grown considerably over the past two decades, allowing individuals to direct their investments to areas that have major positive social impact. RSF is an example.[165]

There is a trend toward supporting and enhancing the capacity of anchor institutions within their communities. Universities, hospitals, and other large institutions have the ability to direct their hiring and purchasing practices away from large national distributors or distance commuters, to focus on concentrating those economic activities closer to home. Networks of anchor institutions can provide enough buying capacity to enable a local distributor to lower its own prices and become more competitive, as well as ensuring that jobs are kept local and not outsourced. Groups, such as, the Democracy Collaborative through their Community Wealth Building Initiatives, are guiding communities to learn how to focus their resources into local, sustainable investment.[166]

Credit Unions[167] are having a major impact on building local investment in all areas of the world. Projects like the Rural Microfinance Technical Assistance Project in Mexico target smaller towns, especially with high areas of indigenous and other marginalized groups. With credit unions being member/customer owned and controlled, and because of the nature of their capital structure, they are able to have lower interest rates on loans, as well as higher interest on savings. Supporting local credit unions and moving from larger banks to consumer-owned credit institutions will increase accountability and divert funds and investments to shared enterprises and neighborhoods.

Internet mechanisms for crowd funding and financing allow for swift responses and smaller levels of investment to generate new, innovative and entrepreneurial businesses. Unreasonable Group, for example, focuses on leveraging resources for entrepreneurs throughout the world who need additional capital to expand their generally green based and right sized technologies to resolve many of the issues facing the world today.

## *Small Business and Cooperatives*

Supporting small local business owners, local distribution hubs, and cooperative investment enhances the shift to a more synergistic economy. The best examples of this exist in developing countries such as Mexico and Peru where individuals meet the purely small competition criteria by becoming licensed money exchange venders (Peru), combi drivers, small shop owners, and small taxi owners and drivers (tuk-tuks/mototaxis).

Business hubs and relationships are being built that connect individuals to one another. Farm to school or restaurant hubs, local farmers' markets, all build a sense of shared community and purpose. Increasingly purchasing and distribution hubs are being built that allow local fisheries and agricultural producers to sell their produce to local markets, including schools, restaurants, and individuals. Some examples include the Kitchen, Sea2Table, and Local Food Hubs like Valley Food Partnership in Montrose and Valley Food Coop in the San Luis Valley of Colorado.[168]

In addition to collaborative financial investment and local hiring and purchasing, the promotion of cooperatives and other shared ownership mechanisms enhances shared, local control as well as higher incomes and productive capacity. The Mondragon Cooperatives (Basque Country, Spain) are perhaps the most recognized model of successful shared ownership. Many local support agencies exist to promote

### *Growing Underground*

Growing Underground is supported by the Unreasonable Group and produces salads, herbs, and leafy greens in converted WWII air raid shelters under the streets of London. This is an example of a sustainable hydroponic farm that leverages advanced LED lighting and precision agriculture to grow high quality greens in a virtually closed-loop system. Systems like Growing Underground use about 1/3 less water than traditional farming methods and are able to use substantially more renewable energy.[169]

### *Building Strong Local and Regenerative Communities*

The Valley Food Partnership near Montrose, Colorado is a coalition of over 50 community groups working to increase local food distribution, healthy eating, and vibrant community relationships.[169]

and provide capacity for the development of cooperatives. For example, the Rocky Mountain Farmer's Union Co-Op Development Center has allowed not only small agricultural producers to create collaboratives but also build cooperatives for nanny services and an interpreters guild.[170] These allow individuals to reap directly the product of their own labor rather than having to go through a third or fourth party who ultimately takes a larger share of the funds.

Possibilities exist for non-money centered exchange that allow for more relationship building and the direct exchange of commodities, time, and resources. Non-monetary economic activity creates less objectification of the individuals and groups involved.

Time banks allow for individuals to share their gifts and talents by trading with other individuals for their abilities. Sophisticated online exchanges allow people to offer their work (anything from lawn care to database management and web design) for the work of another. This works outside of the normal monetary exchange and enables sophisticated bartering of one's work. Two examples of such exchanges include Time Banks[171] and Hour World.[172]

Another alternative exists through the development of local currencies and mutual credit currencies. Local communities can develop currencies that, while not replacing the national currency, allows for an alternative that is able to put productive resources to work more quickly than the primary currencies. Some examples of this include the Brixton Pound in the UK,[173] BerkShares in the US,[174] and Salt Spring Dollars in Canada.[175] Mutual exchanges can include time banking and allow for credit and debit interactions without the actual exchange of the local national currency.

Communities, both local and international, can rely on processes that put market pressure on entities that are proven to engage in practices that are economically or socially irresponsible. Boycotts, disinvestment, sustainable consumption can all be brought into play to shift the way that corporations, businesses, and governments act within society.

Practices should be supported that provide for regenerative and sustainable systems (water, soil, and other ecological networks.) This includes more deliberative and intentional local development, sustainable architecture and urban design, and regenerative community. Denver, Colorado and other communities have recently passed green roof initiatives that increase the amount of greenspace. The concept of regenerative economies is an important one. Much of our ecological integrity has been decreased to such an extent that sustainability requires not only good practices, but processes that actually restore our systems and environment to a healthy state. It will take years, for example, to rebuild the quality of our soil infrastructure through regenerative processes that allow for soil organisms and internal chemistry to create the balance necessary for vibrant crop production.

Mechanisms are needed that build spiritual/inner capital and shift our focus from employment to vocation. How do we shift from human beings as units of production, inputs similar to minerals and wood, to the ultimate end of production being fulfilled human beings? Writers such as Parker Palmer and others are inviting us to see our work as a deeply held vocation to which we are called to find meaning and deep purpose in our lives. The Lilly Endowment's Programs on the Theological Exploration of Vocation (PTEV) has researched the concept of vocation and identified powerful ways in which educators can shift the paradigm from jobs to vocation. This involves shifting our language to one of purpose and meaning, building shared learning communities that support students and each other in discernment around work and money, and building ongoing reflective spaces for guiding us in our journeys toward meaning, service, and personal transformation.

We must also begin to explore different vocational paths. Currently, there is a strong emphasis on college education which often results in significant debt on the part of young people, without a corresponding increase in salary. Communities are beginning to explore "middle skill" options that allow for quality jobs/vocations with good career paths and reliable income.[176]

A final component of vocational shift and right relationship is the building of platforms for deeper conversations around our relationship to money. The capacity of the average citizen to make thoughtful choices is hampered by systems that have encouraged and, to some extent, required, the accumulation of debt. There is a growing movement within churches and other institutions to engage in conversation around the right use of resources and practical ways to begin to get a handle on one's own financial situation. By showing ways to shift one's habits and focus, and through shared support networks, individuals are working themselves out of the suffocating sense of debt and the inability to make proactive decisions around how their money is directed and used.

To move to a truly synergistic economy, we must focus our efforts first locally, and then build networks of networks that learn from each other and rely on mutually beneficial exchange. Local decisions, involving the participation of all members of the community, create a sense of agency, where everyone is able to understand the value of their personal gifts in creating a healthy, loving community.

# Chapter 5
# The Way Forward

*"Never doubt that a small group of thoughtful committed citizens can change the world. Indeed, it is the only thing that ever has".*

—Margaret Mead[177]

## Summary

Our current Money-Centered Economy is producing some dangerous, unsustainable trajectories both for people and Earth that are driven by its focus on unlimited growth. An Oxfam report showed that in 2017 the richest one percent captured 82 percent of the wealth created, while the poorest 50 percent of the world's population got nothing.[178]

The midyear 2018 UN report on extraction of primary resources, including fossil fuels, metals and other materials, documented a tripling of tonnages in just four decades with the richest countries consuming 10 times more than the poorest countries.[179] A major World Wildlife Fund study has recently determined that humanity has wiped out 60 percent of the global animal population since 1970.[180] This stream of bad news has continued with the latest UN report on climate change describing a strong risk of crisis by 2040.[181]

So what are we to do? Typical reactions to this amount of alarming news can include denial: "it's a hoax"; despair: "we are doomed"; or it will be OK: "technology will save us" (*Figure 8, p. 78*). This range of reactions is prompted by the underlying assumption that we would have to make some very uncomfortable adjustments in our lifestyles in order to change the direction in which we are headed.

Figure 8: Climate Change Skeptic[182]

However, a positive, pro-active reaction is possible: we can pursue Quality of Life rather than Quantity of Stuff. Chapter 1 outlined an alternative vision of a Life-Centered Economy that represents a shift from the present growth-oriented economic lens to a moral lens. This vision focuses on how we spend the time of our lives to reach our highest potential as human beings. We can be changemakers for a new economic system that features fairness and sustainability.

In Chapter 2, this vision is imagined as a Life-Centered Economy that relies on economic synergism. Economic synergism can be conceptualized as all of the stakeholders, including the ecosystem, operating in concert for the greater good. The motto of the Life-Centered Economy is "Time is Life," replacing "Time is Money," the motto of the current system. The foundational precepts of the new system are:

- Time over Money
- Quality over Quantity
- Sustainability over Depletion
- Human Potential over Human Exploitation
- Small Scale over Large Scale

In Chapter 3, the human household is used as a focal point and shows the practical potential for economic synergism among the basic components of an economic system:

- Food
- Shelter
- Utilities
- Material goods
- Transportation
- Communication
- Financial choices
- Labor supply
- Money usage

Chapter 4 outlines approaches for the transition to a Life-Centered Economy. These paths for change may build on the positive aspects of the current system, but the shift toward a more ethical model can arise in parallel to it and eventually displace any harmful elements. The potential of emerging processes is highlighted, noting the need for sustainable design with control at the lowest societal level possible with a shift from "jobs" to "fulfilling vocation." Examples are provided of activities already well underway, many of which feature re-localization and community. Tools and resources that enable these changes are identified. A global movement is needed that links a network of networks.

## Our Challenge

The post-World War II economic boom delivered relatively stable jobs to many people and provided company health and retirement benefits for a full generation or more. More people than ever before were able to attend colleges with manageable tuition and housing costs. Many were able to afford a mortgage and move into a house relatively early in their working careers between 1950 and 1980. Prosperity was by no means universal, though. Millions of people were left out of the post-war prosperity by segregation and historical poverty. Still, the civil rights movement held out hope for ever-widening opportunity for all.

There was cause for optimism. During that period, the level of inequality as measured by the income share of the top 10 percent was the lowest in the history of the U.S. (*Figure 9*).[183]

Figure 9. Inequality in the U.S. as measured by the income share of the top 10 percent.[184]

Contrast the scenario of the 1950s through the 1970s with the challenges of today. Income and wealth inequalities in the U.S. have reverted to the levels of the 1930s. If young people are college graduates, they have most likely accumulated significant debt—an average of $37,000/borrower for the class of 2016. The default rate approaches 40 percent but there is no bankruptcy protection for student loans.[185] Perhaps due to these conditions, a survey found that more than one-third of college students struggle with insecurity of both food and housing.[186] On graduation, many are underemployed due to a combination of global outsourcing, automation, and company focus on profit maximization by keeping many workers on a part-time status with little or no health and retirement benefits.

The malaise extends to much of the general economy, cutting across the age spectrum. A recent report showed that 52 percent of workplace tasks would be performed by machines in 2025, up from 29 percent in 2018. While it is expected that new human jobs may more than offset this change, only about one-third of the responding companies planned to re-skill their at-risk workers.[187] We still have a large number of Americans that live pay-check to pay-check. A recent survey found that 40 percent of Americans could not handle a $400 emergency out of savings, without borrowing or selling something.[188]

While the US, with less than five percent of the world population, consumes about 25 percent of its natural resources, the rest of the world has been short-changed in terms of material resources due to our disproportionate consumption. And to compound the problem, we are faced with unsustainable drawdown of non-renewable natural resources, along with planet-destroying pollution from their use. We cannot credibly say to other countries, "We've got ours, good luck to you," or urge them to disproportionately cut back on pollution. So we here in the US really have an obligation to lead the way back from the rampant materialism that our advertising has promoted throughout the world, and to set an example that promotes "Quality of Life" over "Quantity of Stuff."

Human beings built the current economic system, and so human beings can change it. It is not based on some law of nature, like gravity. In fact, the economic system operates against some natural laws like entropic limits. Entropy is a measure of disorder. The second law of thermodynamics states that in a closed system with any of change of energy to another form, or motion of matter, entropy increases. This means that without an introduction of energy, disorder tends to increase.

Three fundamental concepts for an ethical foundation of ecological economics are membership, householding and entropic thrift.

1) Membership implies that humans are members, not masters, of the community of life.

2) Householding means that in deriving our own lives from other living systems, these systems must be respected and maintained.

3) Entropic thrift recognizes natural thermodynamic limits of resources, that lead to scarcity, and so require wise use and just sharing.[189]

We need to reconcile our notion of "liberty" with a just human-nature relationship and our individual agency with responsible self-direction that honors ecological constraints.

The concept of entropic limits has been elaborated on by Kenneth Boulding, an early ecological economist. When materials such as metal ores are extracted from Earth, some is manufactured into products and some goes to waste, but all is dispersed over the surface of Earth. As the finite stocks are used, the potential for additional quantities is diminished. Likewise, in disposing of wastes Earth can only absorb so much naturally, and the excess of harmful chemicals can threaten living systems.[190]

The same analysis applies to the extraction and burning of fossil fuels. As their use continues, the potential remaining for future use diminishes and the pollution of the atmosphere increases, which is driving climate change. Sunlight, as Boulding notes, is the only form of energy that can be considered inexhaustible. If implemented in a timely way, renewable energy from sunlight is an alternative to the fossil fuel depletion and pollution problem.[191]

Regarding materials, Boulding suggests that technology be directed toward using some of the non-renewable materials (while they are still available) to aid in developing closed-cycle manufacturing systems (that reuse "waste" rather than disperse it) and biologically based substitute materials.[192] Interestingly, there are now some encouraging initiatives to produce high-tech plant-based materials. One is to add "nanoplatelets" of vegetable waste to strengthen concrete with reduced amounts of cement, thereby reducing the carbon dioxide emissions from cement production. Another is compressing wood waste into a strong composite that can serve as an alternative to structural plastics and light-weight titanium alloys for aerospace applications.[193]

Finally, Boulding notes that our resource of human knowledge expands as it spreads. The source of the knowledge is not diminished when recipients obtain the knowledge, and so this human process represents a fantastic resource potential.[194]

## *Need for a Morally Grounded Transition*

Perhaps we can empower ourselves to turn away from the destructive path we seem to be following, both for people and planet, through engaging our hearts as well as our minds. As we consider these daunting challenges, we can practice "heartfulness" along with "mindfulness." There is a remarkable feature of generosity or pro-sociality, that evolved in humans and was likely crucial in our survival as a species. It begins manifesting itself around the age of five when children become more aware that generosity is good for their reputation.[195]

While present-day American society emphasizes individualism and competition, we also have a long history of cooperation and we need to lift this up and shift focus from "me" to "we". We truly are all in this together as we try to live within our planetary boundaries by treating both human and other ecosystem life with respect.

In her article describing a rural childhood, Sara Smarsh endorses pride in the work one does, that touches on the myth of the American Dream, that if you work hard enough you will achieve more monetary wealth. But she later recognized that the poor are likely to stay poor under our system. She reminds us that the simple things in life can be satisfying, and that some do not even know how their food is produced.[196]

Even those who have benefited from the current system may still remember the simpler lifestyle of childhood with fondness. This perspective can be used to resist the glorification of workaholics, such as, Elon Musk who works

120 hours per week despite having five children. How does he have time for them? Studies show that too much time and intensity of work does not lead to wellbeing.[197]

With some introspection, can we come to value ourselves by who we are and what we stand for, not what we do or how rich we are? Can we overcome the distractions of media and consumption to reclaim the time of our lives, and our sense of place and community? This is not only possible but would be rewarding in terms of our own wellbeing.

We can use our common sense to find common ground with the many others who recognize the compelling need for change. Some of our commonalities may be:

Fairness: equitable sharing and stewardship of natural resources

Long-term rather than short-term focus: valuing future generations as equal to, rather than less than, ours

Time to reflect on life rather than speeding through it: relationships with friends and family, and development of our highest potential "An unexamined life is not worth living."[198]

# Changes for the Good

## Systemic Impacts

Systems analysis is a methodology widely used to study complex subjects, such as the relationship between economic growth and sustainability. In this case, connections are shown for a wide range of relevant factors, such as material usage, energy consumption, social behavior, environmental pollution, financial resources, and so on. An overview can be depicted for illustration as three overlapping circles representing the economy, society and the environment, which in turn is bounded within a "collective circle" of sustainability. A key takeaway is that individual contributions lie in the "sweet spot," where the circles representing the economy, environment and society intersect in a common area, and thus can have influence on even a large, complex system. This can be interpreted in two ways: 1) individuals can be members of groups, or collectives, that promote sustainability and 2) individuals' self-motivated actions for sustainability can together create an informal autonomous collective that supports sustainability.[199]

## *Viable Transition Paths*

In the book *Enough is Enough* a list of approaches is offered for a shift that originates from people's personal values toward a grassroots rejection of mindless consumption:

- Turn marketing on its ear: employ the well-honed advertising methods towards true wellbeing rather than more stuff.
- Harness the power of art: art can inspire people to imagine the better world we seek.
- Be the change: we can begin "living our values" through buying locally and participating in community initiatives that foster sustainability.
- Recruit influential individuals: their pivotal positions in key organizations and social networks can multiply their influence many times over.
- Juxtapose rampant consumerism with a non-materialistic good life: some aspects of the Transition Town movement could be used in this regard.
- Eliminate planned obsolescence: refuse to buy short-lived products where possible.
- Limit advertising: ad-blockers on electronic devices can help, as well as limits on TV for children.
- Cultivate non-consumerist institutions: support co-ops, land trusts and community work shops.[200]

Specific actions to address climate change could include 1) resistance to new fossil fuel projects, 2) promoting local community commitment to 100 percent renewable energy, and 3) divesting from investments in fossil fuel companies.[201]

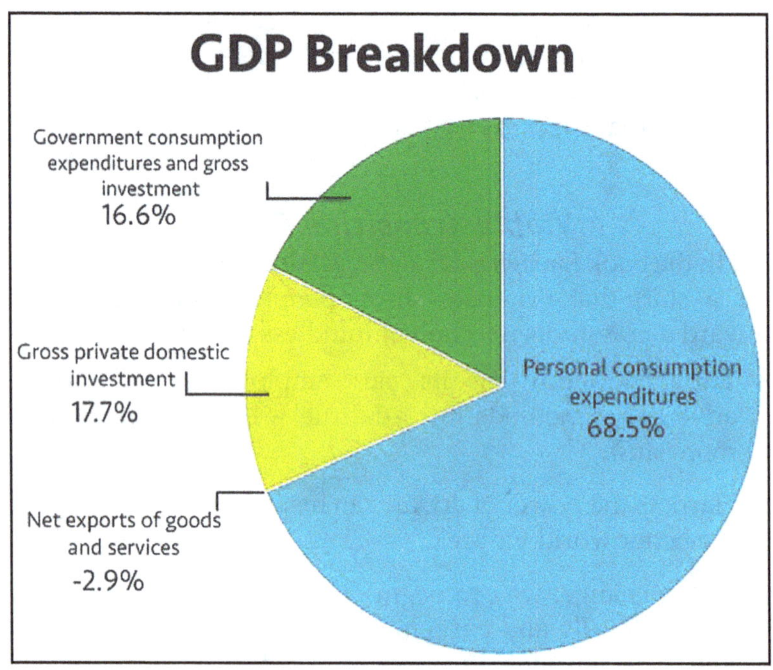


Figure 10. Breakdown of GDP[202]

## *Mindful Consumption*

With about 70 percent of the US economy dependent on consumer demand, we can make a significant impact both individually and collectively in transforming our current over-consumption (*Figure 10*). This is an area where we can utilize the efficiency of the marketplace in responding to a redirection of demand—from "the next new thing" toward sustainable needs-based purchases.

In the 2019 *National Green Pages*, published by Green America, we are urged to "vote with our dollars" to support our values. It is pointed out that purchasing from conventional corporations may support:

- sweatshop labor
- worsening climate change
- child enslavement
- predatory financial practices
- environmental racism
- exposure to toxic chemicals

- political lobbyists
- environmental destruction

If instead, you provide for your needs from certified green businesses with fair trade in mind, you will support:

- nontoxic products
- farming that restores the soil and climate
- living wages and healthy working conditions
- good, green jobs
- social and environmental justice
- lifting up factory and farm workers
- independent green businesses[203]

We of course cannot research our every purchase, but with relatively little effort in checking out "green sources," considering the geographical distance the product must travel, and noting its composition and packaging, we can bring mindfulness and heartfulness to our consumption habits. When we discuss this approach with our friends, family and circles of community we can unleash a multiplier effect. This is an area where we truly can exert some power to change the system for the better.

Probably the most important consumer action we can take is just to buy less of everything. We can go back to enjoying fruit and vegetables as being special when in season, knowing it will come again next year, rather than buying imports from around the globe in off-season. Likewise, a simple rule of thumb for articles of clothing is to give the old item to charity when a new item of that type is bought—and more importantly to consider whether we really need that new item before buying it. We really do not need to upgrade our electronic devices to be "cool" and then spend time mastering all the new bells and whistles, and already there are trends in delaying smartphone replacements.[204] This same principle can apply to other equipment such as appliances and autos, and perhaps is better thought of as voluntary simplicity rather than frugality.[205] A side benefit of examining our true consumption needs is money saved to provide more financial security.

## *The Way Forward*

*"Forces beyond your control can take away everything you possess except one thing, your freedom to choose how you will respond to the situation."*

—Viktor E. Frankl[206]

In his lyrical article, "The Fierce Urgency of How," Peter Buffett provides a brief overview of humanity's journey from thousands of years of communal society to today's "seemingly intractable structure of power and control... in which we are pillaging like hungry ghosts." He notes that what began as a need for survival to accumulate for future consumption has taken on a life of its own. We aimlessly search for meaning in the things we buy, while depleting essential planetary resources that our children will need.[207]

Throughout the evolution of our civilization, technology has been a helper. Now it has reached a stage where it has the capability to bring us together. But like all new tools it has a negative potential—to separate us from each other and the ecosystem. Buffett notes that the more power becomes concentrated, the more it is susceptible to disruption, and some disruption is already beginning through a wide spectrum of global activism.

We can help create the future we want through our connection to nature and the interdependence of all life, and by choosing cooperation and altruism over the "psychotic logic of the invisible hand and individual opportunism."

Ashoka is an organization devoted to the the development of social entrepreneurs, assuming that everyone could be a "changemaker." Ashoka supports 3500 social entrepreneurs in 93 countries, who are needed because our traditional workplaces are increasingly encroached by machines.[208]

Changemakers are those who see emerging patterns, deal with problems, and organize collective action to adapt as the situation changes. This capability depends on empathy-based living for the good of all. Ashoka believes it is the challenge of our time to make everyone a changemaker, and to do that we need to start young, when we are more naturally disposed to such activity.

Social transformation is rooted in personal transformation, and Ashoka wants to restore a universal sense of personal agency, a quality of empowerment that many people do not even see. If the millions of people who do not feel they can take control of their own lives could experience love and respect in action, it really could change the world.[209]

Some practical steps toward positive change begin with a recognition that the workplace is losing its centrality in our self-identification. As large businesses reduce meaningful jobs in terms of both content and security, we can turn instead to rebuilding local community as the economic focus. This approach has four distinct advantages:

1) **No part of the process is wasted.** Even if an economic structure is not achieved as envisioned, skills will have been built and a groundwork laid for future initiatives.

2) **Most steps in the process are pleasant.** It fosters non-hierarchal social engagement, rather than a lot of structured meetings.

3) **The process is open to everyone.** This provides for an eclectic mix of skills, knowledge and points of view. It also paves the way for group buy-in to the initiative.

4) **You do not need anyone's permission.** These new approaches can grow in parallel to existing economic structures, and when proven to be more beneficial, can replace them.

This approach could address the pervasive discontent felt "by people who have been led to believe that their identity and validity arise from the jobs they do, only to discover that there are no jobs at all, or only jobs that no self-respecting person would want to take."[210]

So how do we find sustainable happiness, if economic growth and consumerism cannot deliver it? Happiness can be built on mutually supportive communities that link our wellbeing with that of our neighbors. It also depends on a healthy living Earth, that honors the ecosystem that delivers clean air, fresh water and healthy food.

Sustainable happiness is possible but it does depend on our individual and collective choices. Here are some starting points.

1) **First do no harm:** We need to stop the violence to one another and promote healing—return to the Golden Rule.

2) **Create equity:** Our extreme inequality in economic wealth needs to be dismantled, and Fairness reclaimed as a societal precept.

3) **Value everyone's gifts:** We all have different talents and all are needed. Our goal should be to achieve fulfillment of our highest potential, whatever it may be.

4) **Protect the integrity of the natural world:** We need to engage as components of the ecosystem, not as masters of it, if we are to maintain its vitality for future generations.

5) **Develop practices that support our wellbeing:** We can begin by better attending to our own health through diet and exercise. We can also develop a practice of gratitude and mindfulness. As we focus more on happiness and less on economic growth, we leave time for family, community and many other aspects of our lives that bring true happiness.[211]

Paradoxically, the current system's dependence on consumerism offers a means to transform it. If in our individual practice as consumers, we make "green" life-sustaining choices, both for the things we buy and where we invest, we can help change the economic paradigm. When we link with other like-minded consumers, which is already happening as outlined in Chapter 2, it can bring us toward the needed "tipping point."

In addition to a widespread push for change on an individual basis, there are a host of organizations that are actively pursuing a new economic system similar to the life-centered economy described here but with a variety of different names. So we have concepts like the solidarity economy, the caring economy, the sharing economy, the restorative economy, the regenerative economy, the sustaining economy, the commons economy, the resilient economy and the new economy. As of March, 2017, there were 140 organizations in the New Economy Coalition alone![212]

## Be a Changemaker!

We can all be changemakers, to some degree, for the sustainable world we seek. With heightened awareness we can focus our resources of time and talent in the most effective manner. An interesting perspective is given by the following excerpts from a message attributed to the Elders of the Hopi Nation:

"...It is time to speak your Truth. Create your community. Be good to each other. And do not look outside yourself for the leader.

This could be a good time! ...We are the ones we have been waiting for."[213]

Perhaps the most important thing we could do in exerting our power as consumers is to work toward a national and then a global consumer movement, by linking together individual and small group efforts into a massive refocusing toward sustainable products. There are already many organizations engaged in such like-minded efforts as noted in Chapter 2 and referenced again here.[214]

Social media has received a lot of bad publicity lately due to its subversion by hate groups and the like, but with these guidelines it can offer a great potential for good:

1) Take advantage of interactive activism opportunities in online communities. If you post about a cause you support, your friends and family are more likely to also support it.

2) Make sure your activism is accessible and inclusive. Media activism has a great advantage in accessibility over actions like door-to-door campaigning or showing up for an in-person protest, even though those options can also be supported. An example is given on how the Disability March was organized online by using the successful techniques of the Women's March.

3) Remember that small steps are critical to getting the work done. Even with easy access to online information, it is important to also take small steps like calling your representatives and creating community groups to address key issues. According to the Harvard Business Review, easy to replicate, low-risk tactics are the most likely to succeed.

4) Share the work that other activists are doing. Remembering that we each can't do everything, we can amplify the work of others by spreading it online to our connections.[215]

We can do this! By engaging individually and collectively in our roles as consumers of goods and services, we can achieve a sustainable future that features:

- Product design for re-use or efficient recycle to avoid material waste,
- Video communication replacing much of the transportation for work and leisure,
- Many medical services delivered online at affordable cost,
- Widespread access to free or low cost online education,
- Equitable "gig" economy with co-op platforms and portable benefits,
- 3-D printing for local manufacture of many products,
- Smaller energy-saving housing featuring xeriscape yards or commons,
- Local sharing economy for tools, equipment and cars,
- Plant-based materials replacing non-renewable material resources,
- Time banks and local currencies supplementing national currency, and
- Community-oriented food supply and retail shops.

The prior money-centered economic system will still be operating to some degree in parallel, but its dominance over all of human society and other planetary life and resources will have been broken. Future generations will have been honored, rather than discounted, and will have the gift of a life-centered economic system.

## *Letter from the Future*

We might imagine a letter of gratitude from the future such as the following:

Date: 2050

Location: USA

Dear Grandmother and Grandfather,

Thank you so much for bequeathing us a world that works in concert with nature, and emphasizes the quality of time in our lives rather than money and the quantity of things it can buy. It was your generation that really gave momentum to this transition, especially in the critical 2015 -2025 time frame, and we are so grateful! You chose to conserve our natural resources and save some for us and our future generations, rather than consuming most of what remained for yourselves. We didn't begin our careers burdened with student loan debt. Nor did we suffer from extreme income inequality. Perhaps best of all, you left us the precious legacy of a sustainable planetary ecosystem. And once again each new generation is better off in a true life-sense than the earlier one!

With love and thanks,

Your Granddaughter and Grandson

*"I am only one, but I am one. I cannot do everything, but I can do something. And I will not let what I cannot do interfere with what I can."* —Edward Everett Hale[216]

# *Endnotes*

Websites accessed February 22, 2019.

Full Bibliographic citations for books are in the Bibliography (p. 113).


1) Quaker Institute for the Future <quakerinstitute.org>.
2) Dreby and Lumb, 2012.
3) Alan N. Connor, 2012. <mecteam.blogspot.com/2012/12/restructuring-society-by-alan-n-connor.html>.
4) William Saroyan, 1939, from his award-wining play, *The Time of Your Life.*
5) Wikipedia. 2019. *Life, Liberty, and the Pursuit of Happiness.* <wikipedia.org/wiki/Life,_Liberty_and_the_pursuit_of_Happiness>.
6) Amy Patterson Neubert , 2018. <purdue.edu/newsroom/releases/2018/Q1/money-only-buys-happiness-for-a-certain-amount.html>.
7) Nickerson, 2009, p. 117.
8) Polyp <polyp.org.uk/index.html>.
9) Sarah Van Gelder and the Staff of *YES! Magazine*, Editors, 2014. *Sustainable Happiness.* Oakland: Berrett-Koehler Publishers, pp. 2-4.
10) Fred Magdoff and Chris Williams, 2017. Capitalist Economies Create Waste, Not Social Value. *Monthly Review Press* <truthout.org/articles/capitalist-economies-create-waste-not-social-value>.
11) David Leonhardt, 2017. Lost Einsteins: Innovations We're Missing. *New York Times* <nytimes.com/2017/12/03/opinion/lost-einsteins-innovation-inequality.html>.
12) The column by David Leonhardt describes the research of the Equality of Opportunity Project <opportunityinsights.org>.
13) Wilkinson and Pickett, 2009.
14) Pamela Haines, Ed Dreby, David Kane, Charles Blanchard, 2016 *Toward a Right Relationship with Finance: Debt, Interest, Growth, and Security. QIF Focus Book #9 <quakerinstitute.org>.*
15) Nickerson, 2009.
16) Joy, 2011.
17) Raworth, 2017. pp. 34-44.
18) Raworth, K. 2017. A Doughnut for the Anthropocene: humanity's compass in the 21st century. *The Lancet Planetary Health* 1 (2): 48-49 <thelancet.com/journals/lanplh/articl/PIIS2542-5196(17)30028-1/fulltext#sec1>.
19) Raworth, 2012. A Safe and Just Space for Humanity. *Oxfam Discussion Papers* <oxfam.org/sites/www.oxfam.org/files/dp-a-safe-and-just-space-for-humanity-130212-en.pdf>.

20) Daly, 1994. pp. 155-156.

21) Van Gelder and the Staff of *YES! Magazine*, 2014, pp. 5-7.

22) David Brooks, 2018. *The Power of Altruism* <nytimes.com/2016/07/08/opinion/the-power-of-altruism.html>.

23) Lew Daly and Sean McElwee. Forget the GDP. Some States Have Found a Better Way to Measure Our Progress. *The New Republic* (February 3, 2014).

24) Robert C. Wolcott, 2018. How Automation Will Change Work, Purpose, and Meaning. *Havard Business Review.* <hbr.org/2018/01/how-automation-will-change-work-purpose-and-meaning>.

25) Van Gelder and the Staff of *YES! Magazine*, 2014, pp. 11, 71.

26) John Maynard Keynes, 1930. *Economic Possibilities for our Grandchildren. <marxists.org/reference/subject/economics/keynes/1930/our-grandchildren.htm>.*

27) BBC, 2012. *Global Resources Stock Check.* <bbc.com/future/story/20120618-global-resources-stock-check>.

28) David Korten, 2014. *Change the Story, Change the Future: A Living Economy for a Living Earth Economics of Sustainability: Emerging Models for a Healthy Planet.* Praxis Peace Institute Conference. <davidkorten.org/changethestory-changethefuture/>.

29) Roddy Scheer and Doug Moss. Earthtalk, Scientific American. <scientificamerican.com/article/american-consumption-habits>.

30) Jon Slater, 2016. Sixty-two People Own the same as Half the World. *Davos Report, Oxam* <oxfam.org/en/pressroom/pressreleases/2016-01-18/62-people-own-same-half-world-reveals-oxfam-davos-report>.

31) Lawrence Mishel and Jessica Shicder, 2016. Stock Market Headwinds Meant Less Generous Year for Some CEOs. Economic Policy Institute <epi.org/publication/ceo-and-worker-pay-in-2015>.

32) <cloudfront.crimethinc.com.assets/books/work/images/work-poster-large.jpg>.

33) Richard D. Wolff, 2015. Critics of Capitalism Must include Its Definition. *Turthout.* <truth-out.org/news/item/30678-critics-of-capitalism-must-include-its-definition> p.5.

34) Geoff Mulgan, 2013. Time Rather Than Money. Globalist Bookshelf. <theglobalist.com/time-rather-than-money>.

35) Gwendolyn Hallsmith and Bernard Lietaer, 2011. *Creating Wealth.* Gabriola Island, British Columbia: New Society Publishers, pp. 58-59.

36) Ralph Waldo Emerson, *Ode*. <internal.org/Ralph_Waldo_Emerson/Ode>.

37) David S. Abraham, 2015. The Next Resource Shortage. *New York Times* <nytimes.com/2015/11/20/opinion/the-next-resource-shortage.html?_r=0>.

38) Vince Beiser, 2016. The World's Disappearing Sand. *New York Times* <nytimes.com/2016/06/23/opinion/the-worlds-disappearing-sand.html>.

39) McDonough and Braungart, 2002.

40) Mark Berman, 2016. Former Coal CEO Sentenced to a Year in Prison after 2010. West Virginia Coal Mine Disaster. *Wasington Post* <washingtonpost.com/news/post-nation/wp/2016/04/06/former-coal-ceo-sentenced-to-a-year-in-prison-for-2010-west-virginia-coal-mine-disaster/?utm_term=.b4bd4257bf69>.

41) Deming, 2000.

42) Planet of the Phones. *The Economist* <economist.com/leaders/2015/02/26/planet-of-the-phones>.

43) Coming Together for Change. *Consumers International*. <consumer-sinternational.org>.

44) Green America <greenamerica.org>.

45) Shareable, 2017, and Sundararajan, 2016.

46) Carolyn Said, 2019. Revolt of the Gig Workers: How Delivery Rage Reached a Tipping Point. San Francisco Chronicle <sfchronicle.com/business/article/Revolt-of-the-gig-workers-How-delivery-rage-13605726.php?utm_source=email&utm_medium=email&utm_content=newsletter&utm_campaign=sfc_baybriefing_am>.

47) Nathan Schneider, 2018. Everything for Everyone: The Radical Tradition that is Shaping the Next Economy. Nation, September 2018. <nathanschneider.info/books/everything-for-everyone>.

48) US Department of Energy, 2012. *Additive Manufacturing: Pursuing the Promise.* <eere.energy.gov/manufacturing/pdfs/additive_manufacturing.pdf>.

49) A Printed Smile. *The Economist.* <economist.com/news/science-and-technology/21697802-3d-printing-coming-age-manufacturing-technique-printed-smile>.

50) Habitat for Humanity, *Habitat for Humanity Tops Builder 100 List for Private US Homebuilders* <habitat.org/newsroom/2016/5-25-Habitat-for-Humanity-ranked-top-private-home-builder>.

51) Leslie Thatcher and Rachel Knaebel, 2016. Building an Environmentally Sound House Cheaply, in a Week. <truth-out.org/news/item/38376-building-an-environmentally-sound-house-cheaply-in-a-week>.

52) Schumpeter's Creative Destruction. *Wikipedia. <wikipedia.org/wiki/Creative_destruction>*.

53) Mark Bittman, 2016. G.M.O/ Labeling Law Could Stir a Revolution. *New York Times.* <nytimes.com/2016/09/02/opinion/gmo-labeling-law-could-stir-a-revolution.html>.

54) Zhiwa, Woodbury, 2015. After Paris: Making the Case for a People-powerd Transition to a New Climate Culture. *Truthout.org.* <truth-out.org/opinion/item/34034-after-paris-making-the-case-for-a-people-powered-transition-to-a-new-climate-culture>.

55) *Economist,* Februrary 26, 2016. *The Truly Personal Computer.* <economist.com/news/

briefing/21645131-smartphone-defining-technology-age-truly-personal-computer).

56) Arun Sundararajan, 2016.

57) Benefit Corporations and Certifield B Corps. <benefitcorp.net/businesses/benefit-corporations-and-certified-b-corps>

58) David Gelles, 2016. Investors Want More Firms to Be More Open. This Nonprofit Is Trying to Make It Happen. <nytimes.com/2016/11/15/business/dealbook/dealbook-investing-sustainability-environmental-impact.html>.

59) van Agtmael and Bakker, 2016.

60) Grassroots Economic Organizing <geo.coop>.

61) Seeds of a Good Anthropocene <goodanthropocenes.net>.

62) Local Futures <localfutures.org>.

63) The Power is in Your Hands. *Green America,* Spring 2015, p.3.

64) Flaccavento, 2016, p. 81.

65) Sofia Faruqi, Eriks Brolis, Andrew Wu, 2017. *The Nature Conservancey.* <global.nature.org/content/growing-trees-and-growing-profit-is-your-business-a-restoration-enterprise>.

66) Fair World Project, 2014. <fairworldproject.org/wp-content/uploads/2014/07/Food_Farming_Climate_Change-8x11.jpg>.

67) "The Cost of Eating Cows," *Green American*, Fall 2017, pp.12-13.

68) Natural Resources Defense Council, 2012. Wasted: How America Is Losing up to 40 Percent of its Food from Farm to Fork to Landfill <assets.nrdc.org/sites/default/files/wasted-2017-executive-summary.pdf.>

69) Sharable, 2017.

70) Home Share Colorado. <sunshinehomeshare.org>.

71) Embassy Network. <embassynetwork.com>.

72) Cradle to Cradle Products, Innovation, Institute, 2017. Want to Design Circularity? Consider Your Buildiings as Future Material Banks from the Start. <c2ccertified.org/news/article/want-to-design-for-circularity-consider-your-buildings-as-future-material-b>.

73) McDonough Braungart Design Chemistry (MBDC), 2017. MBDC Apploads Walmart's Encouragement of Cradle toCradle Certified Products. <mbdc.com/2017/11>.

74) Community Wealth. *Community Land Trusts.* <community-wealth.org/strategies/panel/clts/index.html>.

75) Paulette Perhach, 2016. Future House:3-D Printed and REady to Fly. *New York Times* <nytimes.com/2016/07/21/us/future-house-3-d-printed-and-ready-to-fly.html>.

76) A Bridge to the Future. *Economist.* <economist.com/technology-quarterly/2015/09/03/a-bridge-to-the-future>.

77) Tyler Koslow, 2017. 35 Greatest 3D Printed Houses and Structures <all3dp.com/1/3d-printed-house-homes-buildings-3d-printing-construction/>.

78) Habitat for Humanity. <habitat.org/impact/our-work>.

79) Daniel Lerch, p. 302.

80) Maurie J. Cohen, 2017. *Building the New Economy: The Suburban Phase.* <shareable.net/blog/building-the-new-economy-the-suburban-phase>.

81) American Gas Association.*Energy Efficiency—National Gas Utilities.* <aga.org/policy/environment/energy-efficiency-natural-gas-utilities>.

82) Jacques Schonek, 2013. How Big are Power Line Loses? <blog.schneider-electric.com/energy-management-energy-efficiency/2013/03/25/how-big-are-power-line-losses>.

83) Clark Howard, 2019. Five Ways to Make your Old House as Energy-efficient <clark.com/homes-real-estate/5-ways-to-make-your-old-house-as-energy>.

84) Marc Gunther, 2016. Tomorrowland, Today, *Sierra*, May/June 2016, pp.37-40.

85) Marlene Cimons, 2014. *Live Science.* Keeping Up with the Greens: Neighbors Can Spur Conservation. <livescience.com/49165-neighbor-energy-bills-spur-greener-habits.html>.

86) Emerson, Urry, 2017. Solar Creates Mmore US Electricity Jobs Than Oil, Gas, Coal, Nuclear Combined. <truth-out.org/news/item/39738-doe-report-solar-creates-more-us-electricity-jobs-than-oil-gas-coal-nuclear-combined?tmpl=component&print=1>2>.

87) Tracy Matsue Loffelholz and Chris Winters, 2017. *YES! Magazine*, Fall 2017, pp. 20-21.

88) Diane Cardwill, 2017. Solar Experiment Lets Neighbors Trade Energy Among Themselves. *New York Times* <nytimes.com/2017/03/13/business/energy-environment/brooklyn-solar-grid-energy-trading.html>.

89) Aldo Svaldi, 2016. Guzman Energy Promises Renewable Power to the People. *Denver Post* <https://www.denverpost.com/2016/09/04/guzman-energy-promises-renewable-power>.

90) Kailey Kimsa, 2017. Community Solar is Creating Landscapes. *Grassroots Economic Organizing.* Relocalize the Power—Community Energy Solutions Part II. <geo.coop/blog/relocalize-power-community-energy-solutions-part-ii>. (This is a blog, scroll down to this article.)

91) Shareable, 2017, p. 140.

92) *Ibid.,* p. 133.

93) Pacific Institute. *Water-Energy Nexus.* <pacinst.org/issues/water-energy-nexus>.

94) Pacific Institute. *WECalc.* <wecalc.org>.

95) Bettina Boxall, 2014. Use Less Water than your Neighbors. You Get a Smiley Face. <articles.latimes.com/2014/mar/03/science/la-sci-sn-behavioral-water-efficiency-20140303>.

96) *The Economist*, February 22, 2014, "The Drying of the West." pp. 6-7.

97) *Consumer Reports,* 2015. How to Cut your Water Use in Half. *Consumer Reports.* <consumerreports.org/cro/magazine/2015/05/how-to-cut-your-water-use-in-half/index.htm>.

98) Wikipedia. Rural Electrification Act. <en.wikipedia.org/wiki/Rural_Electrification_Act>.

99) Leonard, 2010, pp. 45-51.

100) *Ibid.*, pp. 173-176.

101) Caroline Chen and Eleanor Greene, 2017. In Search of Ethical Fashion, *Green American*, Winter 2017, pp. 6-7.

102) McDonough and Braungart, 2002.

103) Shaw Industries, 2016. <mbdc.com/project/shaw-industries>.

104) *The Globalist: Rethinking Globalization.* The Rise of Plastic: The Past, Present and Future of Plastic Production. <theglobalist.com/the-rise-of-plastic>.

105) Bill Esler, 2016. Hit List: Materials Expert Names 10 Most Endangered Wood Species. <woodworkingnetwork.com/wood/pricing-supply/ten-most-endangered-wood-species>.

106) Brian X. Chen, 2016. Choosing to Skipe the Upgrade and Care for the Gadget You've Got. *New York Times* <nytimes.com/2016/04/21/technology/personaltech>.choosing-to-skipthe-upgrade-and-care-for-the-gadget-youve-got.html>.

107) Earthworks: Recycle My Cell Phone. Why Recycle? <earthworks.org/campaigns/solutions/recycle-cell-phone/why-recycle>.

108) Marjorie Kelly, 2012. The Good Corporation, *YES! Magazine*, Spring 2012, pp. 46-49.

109) B Corporation (certification) <en.wikipedia.org/wiki/B_Corporation_(certification)>.

110) Honeyman, 2014, pp. 12-14.

111) Shareable, 2017.

112) Jack Ewing, 2017. What Needs to Happen Before Electric Cars Take Over the World. *New York Times* <nytimes.com/2017/12/18/business/electric-car-adoption.html>.

113) Neal E. Boudette, 2016. Automakers prepare for an America That's Over the Whole Car Thing. *New York Times* <nytimes.com/2016/12/22/business/automakers-prepare-america-fewer-cars.html>.

114) Sharable, 2017, p. 70.

115) Ibid., pp. 72-73.

116) Ibid., p. 79.

117) Ibid., p. 76.

118) Ibid., pp. 66-67.

119) Irene Kwan, 2013. Planes, Trains, and Autobombiles: Counting Carbon. *The International Council on Clean Transportation.* <theicct.org/blogs/staff/planes-trains-and-automobiles-counting-carbon>.

120) Paul Lewis, 2017. Our Minds Can Be Hijacked: The Tech Insiders who Fear a Smartphone Dystopia. *The Guardian* <theguardian.com/technology/2017/oct/05/smartphone-addiction-silicon-valley-dystopia>.

121) Umair Haque, 2018. Facebook's Greatest Weapon: Endless Comparison of Ourselves to Others. *The Guardian* <theguardian.com/lifeandstyle/2018/jan/20/facebooks-greatest-weapon-endless-comparison-of-ourselves-to-others?CMP=share_btn_link>.

122) Nina Jankowicz, 2017. The Only Way to Defend Against Russia's Information War *New York Times.* <nytimes.com/2017/09/25/opinion/the-only-way-to-defend-against-russias-information-war.html>.

123) Natasha Bach, 2018. Facebook Has Enlisted the Help of This News Agency to Debunk Fake News During Midterm Elections. *Fortune* <fortune.com/2018/03/08/ap-associated-press-fact-checkers-facebookus-fake-news-midterm-elections>.

124) *US News, 2017.* Efforts Gros to Help Students Evaluate What They See Online. <usnews.com/news/best-states/iowa/articles/2017-12-30/alarmed-by-fake-news-states-push-media-literacy-in-schools>.

125) *The Economist*, January 14, 2017."The Return of the MOOC," pp. 9-12.

126) Natasha Loder, 2017. *The Economist, 1843.* <1843magazine.com/technology/is-there-a-doctor-in-my-pocket>.

127) Ben Tarnoff, 2017. Time to Release the Internet from the Free Market—and Make it a Basic Right. *The Guardian* <theguardian.com/technology/2017/nov/29/net-neutrality-internet-basic-right-america-trump-administration?CMP=share_btn_link>.

128) Scott B. Weingart, The Route of a Text Message, a Love Story. *Motherboard* <motherboard.vice.com/en_us/article/ywnz37/electric-coops-internet-america-cooperatives-broadband>.

129) Farhad Manjoo, 2017. The Alt-Majority: How Social Networks Empowered Mass Protests Against Trump. *New York Times* <nytimes.com/2017/01/30/technology/donald-trump-social-networks-protests.html>.

130) Robertson, 1985.

131) Jeff Spross, 2016. How insane work hours became a mark of American privilege. *The Week* <theweek.com/articles/629256/how-insane-work-hours-became-mark-american-privilege>.

132) Editorial Board, July 14, 2016. How Excessive Executive Pay Hurts Shareholders. *New York Times* <nytimes.com/2016/07/14/opinion/how-excessive-executive-pay-hurts-shareholders.html>.

133) Sharable, 2017. pp. 103-105.

134) *Ibid.*, p. 112.

135) *Ibid.*, p. 110.

136) FAB Lab, MIT. <fabfoundation.org>.

137) Sharable, 2017, pp. 106-107.

138) Gus Speth, *The Joyful Economy* <thenextsystem.org/sites/default/files/2017-08/GusSpeth-1.pdf> pp. 17-18.

139) Hallsmith and Lietaer, 2011. pp. 136-142.

140) Mulgan, 2013, p. 228.

141) David Berrian, 2015. *Debt is Not the Problem*, *YES! Magazine*, Summer 2015, p. 64.

142) Geoff Mulgan, 2013.Time Rather Than Money. *The Globalist.* <heglobalist.com/time-rather-than-money>.

143) Dominguez and Robin, 1992.

144) Local Currencies Program. *Schumacher Center for New Economics,* 2019. <centerforneweconomics.org/content/local-currencies>.

145) Sharable, 2017, p. 240.

146) Jonnelle Marte, 2014. Abount 100 Million Americans Are Now Using Credit Unions. Should You Join Them? *Washington Post* <wapo.st/URMVKH?tid=ss_mail&utm_term=.44685087801b>.

147) Sharable, 2017, p. 237.

148) Ralph Nader, 2018. Corporate Coersion and the Drive to Eliminate Buying with Cash. *Common Dreams* <commondreams.org/views/2018/01/03/corporate-coercion-and-drive-eliminate-buying-cash>.

149) Scott Fullwiler, Stephanie Kelton, Catherine Ruetschlin, and Marshall Steinbaum, 2018. *Macroeconomic Effets of Student Debt Cancellation.* Levy Economics Institute of Bard College. <levyinstitute.org/publications/the-macroeconomic-effects-of-student-debt-cancellation>.

150) Randall Smith, 2016. Investors Sharpen Focus on Social and Environmental Risks to Stocks. *New York Times* <nytimes.com/2016/12/14/business/dealbook/investors-social-environmental-corporate-governance.html>.

151) "Victory at ExxonMobil Shareholder Meeting," *Catalyst*, Summer 2017, p. 6.

152) *As You Sow,* 2017. The 100 Most Overpaid CEOs 2017: Are Fund Managers Asleep at the Wheel? <asyousow.org/reports/the-100-most-overpaid-ceos-2017-are-fund-managers-asleep-at-the-wheel>.

153) Bill McKibben, 2017. Cashing out from the Climate Casino. *New York Times.* <nytimes.com/2017/12/15/opinion/finance-global-warming.html>.

154) Green American, *Socially Responsible Investing.* <greenamerica.org/socially-responsible-investing>.

155) Speth, 2017, pp.17-19.

156) Smith, A., 1990. *Wealth of Nations.* Hoboken, N.J.: EBSCOhost (EBSC).

157) Rifkin, J., 2014. *The Zero Marginal Cost Society.* New York: Palgrave Macmillan.

158) Nonaka, I., & Konno, N. (1998). The Concept of 'Ba': Building a Foundation for Knowledge Creation. *California Management Review,* 40(3), 40-54.

159) National Coalition for Dialogue and Deliberation <ncdd.org>.

160) Participatory Budgeting <participatorybudgeting.org>.

161) Schumacher, E. (1973). *Small is Beautiful: Economics as if People Mattered.* New York: Harper and Row.

162) Calvert Impact Capital. Ours to Own. <ourstoown.org>.

163) Community Resource Center. <crcamerica.org>.

164) Denver Foundation Social Venture Capital Partners <denverfoundation.org/Your-Giving/Collective-Giving/Social-Venture-Partners>.

165) RSF Social Finance <rsfsocialfinance.org/invest/social-investment-fund>.

166) Democracy Collaborative—Builiding Community Wealth. <democracycollaborative.org/content/our-mission>.

167) World Council of Credit Unions <woccu.org>.

168) Valley Food Partnership <valleyfoodpartnership.org>.

169) Growing Underground <growing-underground.com.>

170) Rocky Mountain Farmers Union <rmfu.org/what-we-do/cooperation/co-op-development-center>.

171) Time Banks <timebanks.org>.

172) Hour World <hourworld.org>.

173) Brixton Poung <brixtonpound.org>.

174) BerkShares <berkshares.org>.

175) Salt Spring Dollars <saltspringdollars.com>.

176) J. Brundin, 2019. Does Everyone Need College For High-Paying Jobs? Here's the Middle Skills Option. Colorado Public Radio: <cpr.org/news/story/does-everyone-need-college-high-paying-jobs-heres-middle-skills-option#.dpuf>.

177) This great quote is generally attributed to Margaet Meade, although no one seems to know the source. Perhaps it was in a conversation <quoteinvestigator.com/2017/11/12/change-world>.

178) Oxfam, 2018. *Richest One Percent Captured 82 Percent of the Wealth Created Last Year While the Poor Got Nothing*

<oxfamamerica.org/press/richest-1-percent-captured-82-percent-of-wealth-created-last-year-while-poorest-half-of-the-world-got-nothing>.

179) UN Environment, 2016. Worldwide Extraction of Materials Triples in Four Decades Intensifying Climate Change and Air Pollution. <unenvironment.org/news-and-stories/press-release/worldwide-extraction-materials-triples-four-decades-intensifying>.

180) Damian Carrington, 2018. Humanity Has Wiped Out Sixty Persent of Animal Populations since 1970. <theguardian.com/environment/2018/oct/30/humanity-wiped-out-animals-since-1970-major-report-finds?CMP=share_btn_link.>

181) Coral Davenport, 2018. Major Climate Report Describes a Strong Risk of Crisis as Early as 2040. *New York Times* <nytimes.com/2018/10/07/climate/ipcc-climate-report-2040.html>.

182) Polyp. <polyp.org.uk/index.html>.

183) Saez, Emmanuel and Thomas Piketty, 2003. Income inequality in the United States: 1913–1998. Quarterly Journal of Economics, 118(1), 1–39. Saez and Piketty (2003) and Table A1 in Saez (2007).

184) Saez, Emmanuel, 2007. Table A1: Top fractiles income shares (excluding capital gains) in the US, 1913–2005, data provided by the-Econometrics Laboratory Software Archive <elsa.berkeley.edu/~saez/TabFig2005prel.xls>.

185) Daniela Senderoqicz, 2018. *Yes! Magazine.* Ending the Secrecy of the Student Debt. <truthout.org/articles/ending-the-secrecy-of-the-student-debt-crisis>.

186) Sara Goldrick-Rab, Jed Richardson, Joel Schneider, Anthony Hernandez, and Clare Cady, 2018. Still Hungry and Homeless in College. *Wiscon Hope Lab.* <hope4college.com/wp-content/uploads/2018/09/Wisconsin-HOPE-Lab-Still-Hungry-and-Homeless.pdf>.

187) Rajeshni Naidu-Ghelani, 2018. *Machines Will Do More than Half the Work by 2025.* <cbc.ca/news/business/jobs-of-future-technology-davos-1.4826623>.

188) Sarah O'Brien. 2018. *Fed Survey Shows 40 Percent of Adults Still Can't Cover a $400 Emergency Expense.* <cnbc.com/2018/05/22/fed-survey-40-percent-of-adults-cant-cover-400-emergency-expense.html>.

189) Brown and Timmerman, 2015, p. 284.

190) Boulding, 1964, pp. 141-142.

191) *Ibid.*, pp. 143-144.

192) *Ibid.*, p. 152.

193) *Economist,* 2018. Making Builidngs, Cars, and Planes from Materials Based on Plant Fibres. <economist.com/science-and-technology/2018/06/14/making-buildings-cars-and-planes-from-materials-based-on-plant-fibres>.

194) Boulding, p. 141.

195) Carl Simmer, 2018. Seeking Human Generosity's Origins in an Ape's Gift to Another Ape. *New York Times* <nytimes.com/2018/09/11/science/generosity-apes-bonobos.html>.

196) Sarah Smarsh, 2018. Country Pride: What I Learned Growing up in Rural America. *The Guardian* <theguardian.com/us-news/2018/sep/06/country-pride-kansas-rural-america-sarah-smarsh?CMP=share_btn_link>.

197) Alex Hern, 2018. Will Elon Musk's 120-hour Week Stop Us Worshipping Workaholism. *The Guardian.* <theguardian.com/technology/2018/aug/23/elon-musk-120-hour-working-week-tesla?CMP=share_btn_link>.

198) Quotation attributed to Socrates in *Plato's Apology*.

199) Higgins, 2015. p. 176.

200) Dietz and O'Neill, 2013. pp. 162-164.

201) Jamie Henn, 2018. *Common Dreams.* <comondreams.org/views/2018/01/25/fossil-free-fast-climate-resistance-game-plan-2018>.

202) GDP Breakdown. <static.financialsense.com/historical/users/u3089/images/2016/0217/01-gdp-breakdown.png>.

203) National Green Pages, 2019. *Green America* <greenamerica.org/product/national-green-pages-2019>.

204) Geoffrey A. Fowler, 2018. We've Reached Peak Smartphone. What Are Apple and Samsung Going to Do Now? *Washington Post.* <wapo.st/2nDboUr?tid=ss_mail&utm_term=.2a3eeabb6bcb>.

205) Julia Kagan, 2018. *Voluntary Simplicity*. <investopedia.com/terms/v/voluntary-simplicity.asp>.

206) Frankl, 1946.

207) Peter Buffett, 2018. The Fierce Urgency of How. *Yes! Magazine* <esmagazine.org/happiness/the-fierce-urgency-of-how-20180101>.

208) Ashoka <ashoka.org/en-US/node/31089>.

209) David Brooks, 2018. *Everyone a Changemaker.* <nytimes.com/2018/02/08/opinion/changemaker-social-entrepreneur.html>

210) Monbiot, pp. 89-91.

211) Van Gelder and the Staff of *YES! Magazine*, 2014, pp. 8-9.

212) Speth, 2017. pp.24-25.

213) *From the Elders of the Hopi Nation*, Oraibi, Arizona., 2000. <shambhala.com/images/illus/Prophecy.pdf>.

214) *Consumers International: Coming Together for Change.* <consumersinternational.org>.

215) Alaina Leary, 2018. *Yes! Magazine.* <yesmagazine.org/people-power/yes-social-media-can-be-used-for-positive-change-20180423>.

216) Edward Everett Hale > Quotes <goodreads.com/author/quotes/8183>.

# Bibliography


van Agtmael and Bakker, 2016. *The Smartest Places on Earth: Why Rustbelts Are the Emerging Hot Spots of Global Innovation.* New York: Wiley Online Library <onlinelibrary.wiley.com/doi/abs/10.1111/fcsr.12222>.

Boulding, Kenneth E., 1964. *The Meaning of the 20th Century.* New York: Harper & Row.

Brown, Peter G. and Timmerman, Peter, Eds., 2015. *Ecological Economics for the Anthropocene.* New York: Columbia University Press.

Consumer Activism: Consumers International <consumersinternational.org>, Green America <greenamerica.org>.

Daly, Herman E. and Cobb, Jr., John B. 1994. *For the Common Good.* Boston: Beacon Press.

Deming, William Edwards, 2000. *Out of the Crisis.* Boston MA: The MIT Press.

Dietz, Rob and O'Neill, Dan, 2013. *Enough Is Enough.* San Francisco: Berrett-Koehler Publishers.

Dominguez, Joe and Robin, Vicki, 1992. *Your Money or Your Life.* New York: Viking.

Dreby, Ed, and Judy Lumb, Editors, 2012. *Beyond the Growth Dilemma: Toward an Ecologically Integrated Economy.* QIF Focus Book #6 <quakerinstitute.org>, Caye Caulker, Belize: *Producciones de la Hamaca.*

Flaccavento, Anthony, 2016. *Building a Healthy Economy from the Bottom Up.* Lexington: University Press of Kentucky.

Frankl, Viktor, 1946. *Man's Search for Meaning. An Introduction to Logotherapy.* Republished by Beacon Press, Boston, MA, 2006.

Grassroots Organizing: GEO <geo.coop>, *Seeds of a Good Anthropocene* <goodanthropocenes.net>, *Local Futures* <localfutures.org>.

Hallsmith, Gwendolyn and Lietaer, Bernard, 2011. *Creating Wealth.* Gabriola Island, BC, Canada: New Society Publishers.

Higgins, Karen L., 2015. *Economic Growth and Sustainability.* San Diego: Academic Press/Elsevier.

Honeyman, Ryan, 2014. *The B Corp Handbook.* San Francisco: Berrett-Koehler Publishers.

Joy, Leonard, 2011. *How Does Societal Transformation Happen? Values Development, Collective Wisdom, and Decision Making for the Common Good. QIF Focus Book #4 <quakerinstitute.org>.* Caye Caulker, Belize: *Producciones de la Hamaca.*

Leonard, Annie, 2010. *The Story of Stuff.* New York: Free Press.

Lerch, Daniel, Ed., 2017. *The Community Resilience Reader.* Washington, DC: Island Press.

McDonough, William and Braungart, Michael, 2002. *Cradle to Cradle.* New York: North Point Press.

Monbiot, George, 2017. *Out of the Wreckage.* London: Verso.

Mulgan, Geoff, 2013. *The Locust and the Bee.* Princeton: Princeton University Press.

Nickerson, Mike, 2009. *Life, Money and Illusion. British.* Columbia: New Society Publications.

Raworth, Kate, 2017. *Doughnut Economics.* Vermont: Chelsea Green Publishing.

Rifkin, J., 2014. *The Zero Marginal Cost Society.* New York: Palgrave Macmillan.

Robertson, James, 1985. *Future Work.* England: Gower Publishing. This is out of print but accessible at <jamesrobertson.com>.

Schumacher, E. (1973). *Small is Beautiful: Economics as if People Mattered.* New York: Harper and Row.

Shareable, Eds., 2017. *Sharing Cities: Activating the Urban Commons. Creative Commons.* <shareable.net/sites/default/files/Sharing percent-20Cities.pdf>.

Smith, A., 1776. *Wealth of Nations.* Republished by EBSCOhost, 1990.

Speth, Gus, 2017. *The Joyful Economy.* <thenextsystem.org/sites/default/files/2017-08/GusSpeth-1.pdf>.

Sundararajan, Arun, 2016.*The Sharing Economy.* Cambridge: MIT Press.

van Agtmael, Antoine and Bakker, Fred, 2016. *The Smartest Places on Earth.* New York: Public Affairs.

van Gelder, Sarah & Staff of YES! Magazine, Eds., 2014. *Sustainable Happiness.* Oakland: Berrett-Koehler Publishers.

Wilkinson, Richard and Kate Pickett, 2009. *The Spirit Level: Why Greater Equality Makes Societies Stronger.* New York NY: Bloomsbury Press.

## *Quaker Institute for the Future*

*Advancing a global future of inclusion, social justice, and ecological integrity through participatory research and discernment.*

The Quaker Institute for the Future (QIF) seeks to generate systematic insight, knowledge, and wisdom that can inform public policy and enable us to treat all humans, all communities of life, and the whole Earth as manifestations of the Divine. QIF creates the opportunity for Quaker scholars and practitioners to apply the social and ecological intelligence of their disciplines within the context of Friends' testimonies and the Quaker traditions of truth seeking and public service.

*The focus of the Institute's concerns include:*

• Moving from economic policies and practices that undermine Earth's capacity to support life to an ecologically based economy that works for the security, vitality and resilience of human communities and the well-being of the entire commonwealth of planetary life.

• Bringing the governance of the common good into the regulation of technologies that holds us responsible for the future well-being of humanity and the Earth.

• Reducing structural violence arising from economic privilege, social exclusion, and environmental degradation through the expansion of equitable sharing, inclusion, justice, and ecosystem restoration.

• Reversing the growing segregation of people into enclaves of privilege and deprivation through public policies and public trust institutions that facilitate equity of access to the means life.

• Engaging the complexity of global interdependence and its demands on governance systems, institutional accountability, and citizen's responsibilities.

• Moving from societal norms of aggressive individualism, winner-take-all competition, and economic aggrandizement to the practices of cooperation, collaboration, commonwealth sharing, and an economy keyed to strengthening the common good.



<quakerinstitute.org>

www.ingramcontent.com/pod-product-compliance
Lightning Source LLC
Chambersburg PA
CBHW052043270326
41931CB00012B/2613
* 9 7 8 9 7 6 8 2 7 3 1 1 6 *